libraries ni

Also by Ryan Tubridy

JFK in Ireland

THE
IRISH ARE
COMING

RYAN TUBRIDY

WILLIAM
COLLINS

William Collins
An imprint of HarperCollins*Publishers*
77–85 Fulham Palace Road,
London W6 8JB
WilliamCollinsBooks.com

First published in Great Britain by William Collins 2013

1 3 5 7 9 8 6 4 2

Copyright © Ryan Tubridy 2013

A catalogue record for this book is available from the British Library.

ISBN 978-0-00-731745-5

Typeset in Minion by Birdy Book Design

Printed and bound in Great Britain by Clays Ltd, St Ives plc

MIX
Paper from
responsible sources
FSC
www.fsc.org
FSC™ C007454

For Mum and Dad
Thank you for history, humour and love.

CONTENTS

INTRODUCTION

FOR EIGHT HUNDRED YEARS OR THEREABOUTS, one of history's greatest neighbourhood disputes has been rumbling on between two countries that on the face of it should be best of friends. Separated only by a 130-mile stretch of water, Ireland and Britain have always had what the Americans like to call 'issues'.

Until relatively recently, the Irish considered themselves to be put upon by their nearest neighbour. We felt residual repression and an entitlement to complain about 'eight centuries of hurt'. The British considered the Irish a boozy, noisy and troublesome neighbour but – let's be fair – weren't short of the odd bout of anti-social behaviour themselves. Such clichés are convenient by way of a Ladybird introduction to Anglo-Irish neuroses but they are glib and hide the enormous complexities that lie behind this strange and compulsive relationship. So let's look a little deeper.

Eight hundred is a neat number. Round, even and large, it's the number used when people casually refer to the amount of time Ireland has been annoyed, pestered and occupied by 'the Brits'. For a long time, when someone was asked why we had such a gripe with the British, the retort was simply 'Eight hundred years'. It's unlikely there'll be mention of the Norman invasion of the late

1

twelfth century that marked the start of direct English involvement in Irish affairs but in many respects, that's when the trouble began. Ireland proved a difficult outpost to maintain despite being right on the doorstep because the people tended to be fiercely proud, independent and uncooperative. The more they kicked off, the more the English cracked the whip and so began the rocky road that would last . . . well, eight hundred years.

During the sixteenth and seventeenth centuries, Irish lands were confiscated and plantations created with English bosses in charge. Some were benign and respectful to locals but a lot came and treated the place and the people with contempt, often functioning as absentee landlords, sending in agents to do the dirty work while enjoying the financial rewards from afar. Cromwell was hated for bringing across his soldiers to enforce the law with an iron fist that left a bloody legacy, and when Wolfe Tone led the 1798 rebellion against English rule, he achieved national support. His efforts were fruitless in the short term, but the die was cast for future leaders of an embattled nation.

The famine known as the Great Hunger saw a million Irish dead between 1845 and 1852 and a million more emigrating to America, Australia and Canada, hoping that a new land would bring fresh hope and a bright beginning. The British government response to the famine was scribbled on the back of an envelope too late in the day and then tied up in red tape. In very simple terms, they sat back and tutted as the Irish starved and the population dropped by a quarter (although debate on this issue continues to rage, but that's for another day).

Despite this, Ireland sent the English lots of its best writers and dramatists and in 1914 a whole load of Irish boys headed for London to sign up and fight for King and Country. But two years on, bang in the middle of the First World War, another bunch of Irish boys marched up to Dublin's General Post Office to proclaim a Republic. Within months of that failed 1916 rebellion, the British made martyrs of the leadership by killing them in cold blood and found themselves in the middle of war they could well have done without. That was settled in 1921 and what can only be described as an Anglo-Irish Cold War began – and would last for the best part of the next century.

The lure of television

Throughout the fraught twentieth century, Ireland strove to forge its own identity by pretending that Britain barely existed. This meant doing things on our own terms as a country and not kowtowing to our former masters. We didn't 'do' the Second World War (we even had our own name for it – 'The Emergency') and those who did join the British army were largely ignored or reviled on their return home and have only recently been officially remembered in post-peace-process Ireland.

The Irish might have moaned about the 'bloody Brits' but in the 1950s and 60s they headed to London in their droves when there was lots of building work to be had. There are very few motorways you can drive on, Tube stations you can enter, football stadia you can cheer in, or buildings you can work or live in that haven't felt the trowel of an Irish plasterer or the brush of an Irish painter. It was suitable work for émigrés who weren't particularly educated or qualified but knew how to dig a hole and work hard. They were drawn towards population centres like London, Liverpool, Manchester and Glasgow, but often stayed in their own self-created ghettos – such as London's Cricklewood and Kilburn. Partly this was because the welcome they encountered wasn't the friendliest, with many a boarding house having a 'No blacks, no dogs, no Irish' sign by the front door. However, just as they did in America, the Irish newcomers found their feet, made money and set up homes.

United by war and economics but divided by history and denial, it was the second half of the twentieth century that introduced a third intangible thread that brought these disparate countries together – popular culture. Television would change the day-to-day lives of British citizens first and it wasn't long before the Irish followed suit. By 1955, when the signal was strong enough, Irish television viewers could watch British programmes and suddenly the 'old enemy' was in Irish living rooms. They looked just like us and they had similar worries. Bar the accents, they could've *been* us. What to do now?

It was only a matter of time before the lure of the London limelight became too strong for a slew of Irishmen who watched their televisions in awe as Frankie Howerd, Tony Hancock and Bob Monkhouse strutted their stuff. The small screen offered some local talent the opportunity for big things. A selection of Irish broadcasters, actors and entertainers reckoned they had what it might take to mix it with the best of these guys and so packed their bags, kissed goodbye to a future in Ireland and headed for the streets of London. In many respects, this marked the beginning of a very public association between Irish people and the great British public. The most obvious and recognizable names emerge throughout the 60s and into the 70s and yet these iconic monikers are only one part of a much bigger story and a much deeper relationship.

Anglo-Irish relations deteriorated again with the Troubles of the

70s and 80s. The British looked askance at anyone with an Irish accent and wondered if they had a whiff of sulphur about them, or if they were related to someone who might be troublesome. Then there were the gross injustices of the Birmingham Six and the Guildford Four when people were just picked up off the street and banged away until eventually justice came along. Throughout that time, Terry Wogan was enormously important as a symbol of the civilized Irish. Every morning from 1972 to 1984 people woke to the tones of a cheery Irishman who made them forget about the unrest and reassess their view of the nation, then throughout the 80s he was on their TVs every evening straight after the news. I've always thought Wogan was more important than he's given credit for in terms of tempering the British view of the Irish at a critical time.

The peace process came along in the 1990s, leading up to the Good Friday Agreement of 1998. Sure, there have been ups and downs since but once Queen Elizabeth came to Ireland in 2011 and was seen belly-laughing with a fishmonger in Cork, it seemed clear the Cold War was over and the neighbours were friends at last.

The Irish in Britain

The question this book asks is 'What have the Irish ever done for the UK?' Sit comfortably, because the answer is rather longer than you might realize . . . Who invented the submarine? Who is the cleverest funny man in Britain? Who is the most-loved radio host? Who makes the best hats for royal occasions? Who populates the cast of Harry Potter films? Who raised hell like no others? Who reports from the world's most treacherous hot spots? You know where this is going but you'll have to read on in order to equip yourself with such 'Oh, I never knew that' moments.

From the Duke of Wellington (the man, not the pub) to the Coach and Horses (the hostelry of choice for Richard Harris and Peter O'Toole) and from Eamonn Andrews to Graham Norton, the Irish have served and been served by the UK. This book is intended as a friendly postcard or, at the very least, a yellow Post-it from one neighbour to another with a view to reminding each other of how we've enriched each other's lives, in sickness and in health, for richer and for . . . you get the idea.

I wrote this to celebrate those born in the Republic who came to live in Britain (for a time at least) and made a significant impact on British life.

*   *   *

Inclusion is based on a more or less arbitrary decision-making process by a committee of one, with no discussion and no voting. This is not *Eurovision* or a council election. This is one man's curiosity about two countries that mean so much to each other. I haven't included Bono, who is of course a household name in the UK, because he has always remained resident in Ireland. I haven't included Daniel Day Lewis because he was born in England although he now has Irish citizenship. I haven't included anyone from the North of Ireland because their history of emigration to England and reasons for emigrating are an entirely different story. I'm writing about the country I'm from, and George Best, Kenneth Branagh and Patrick Kielty need a book of their own (maybe some-one will write it one day). Having said all that, I might break my own rules sometimes – but that's the author's prerogative.

For each of the people my committee of one has chosen, I'll be looking at why they came over, how they fared, what the Irish think of them, what the British think of them, and what I personally think of them. In this way, I hope to shine some light on our differences and similarities, our shared quirks and oddities, and the way history has affected our views of each other.

So let's get on with it and endeavour to discover how the Irish really did help to make Britain Great.

1

THE
HELLRAISERS

THE IRISH HAVE A REPUTATION for drinking a lot – and make no mistake, we *do* drink a lot. There's no point being politically correct about it. A 2009 survey found that 54 per cent of Irish adults engage in harmful drinking each year, compared to a European average of just 28 per cent. The oldest pub in Ireland is said to date back to 1198 and the Irish have been drinking ever since, perhaps to help them cope with all those centuries of hurt they blamed the English for. The first written mention of whiskey comes from 1405 and they famously invented the shebeen (Irish: *síbín*), a place where illegal home-brewed booze could be drunk without paying excise duties to the British.

Drinking has always been a sociable thing with the Irish. We don't sit at home nursing a can of Guinness; we're out there with our friends, supping a well-pulled pint and enjoying the craic. The pub is a place where deals are done, tips on the horses are passed along, and generally the world is set to rights. Until fifty or sixty years ago no decent lady would be seen in a pub (many banned them), but I'm delighted to say that the Irish now welcome just as many women in their drinking establishments as men.

When there was a wave of Irish folk emigrating to the UK in the 50s and 60s, it was soon noted that they had a taste for the hard stuff. The Americans had long known the Irish were that way inclined. If they wanted an Irishman in a Hollywood movie in the 1950s, they stuck Bing Crosby in a priest's outfit with a whiskey in his hand. If they wanted an Irishwoman, they chose someone tired-looking, with twenty-five children and a boozy husband. The stereotype stuck for decades as the waves of economic migrants caught the ferry across to British shores.

It wasn't just booze and builders the Irish were exporting to the UK in the 50s and 60s. Some of our home-grown actors fancied playing in front of the bigger, more cosmopolitan audiences of London's West End and making names for themselves in the movies so they sauntered over, complete with their home-grown drinking habits. If they made fools of themselves appearing drunk on chat shows, it was only part and parcel of the world they lived in. Besides, the English had Oliver Reed and the Welsh had Richard Burton, so it's not as though they were drinking alone.

The ones I put into the 'hellraiser' category weren't just boozers, though; they upgraded their drinking until they were completely out there. It was a Gatsby party done three-six-five days a year, and it included plenty of womanizing and sometimes a snort of white powder as well. Yet these were extraordinarily talented men who managed to work hard and play hard. How they were able to hit the tiles and hit the boards at the same time I'll never know, but they lived to a good old age – well, most of them.

Back home the Irish watched with a mixture of pride at the awards ceremonies and horror at the tabloid headlines, but always there was a sense of 'He's one of ours.' And the first two hellraisers I'm going to talk about are legends who completely transcend their boozy reputations because they were simply so amazing at what they did.

RICHARD HARRIS: the excessive-compulsive
1 October 1930–25 October 2002

If I win an award for something I do, the London papers describe me as 'the British actor Richard Harris'. If I am found drunk in a public place, they always refer to me as 'the Irish actor Richard Harris'.

Standing proudly in the south-west of Ireland there's a significant province that reeks of rebellion, tenacity and belligerence. That province is Munster, and within Munster is Limerick, a city that produces paradoxes by the cartload. A rugby city with a large working-class population, there is a celebrated statue that shows two players, arms outstretched, grasping for a ball. One of the players is a docker, the other a doctor. Together they play for the same club, province and (if lucky) country. They work hard, they play hard and they are unconcerned by class. Welcome to the city that gave the world Richard Harris, a city where two classes met and mingled freely.

In fact, Richard Harris's father started out wealthy – he was a flour mill owner – but home life was shattered when the family business fell on hard times and, almost overnight, the cars, maids and gardeners that had populated his life were gone. Harris reflected, 'One day was luxury, the next morning my mother was on her knees scrubbing floors.'

Loss figured regularly in the young Harris's world. A sister's death from cancer deeply affected him and in many ways informed his worldview: 'I wanted to embrace it all. I had a terrible desire to let nothing pass me by.' That desire led to a contrary existence that helped to attract and repel people in equal measure. At home, as one of seven children, he had to make a lot of noise to get heard. At school, the air heavy with testosterone, Harris was first in the queue and back of the class. He set fire to the toilets on one occasion and when a nun rapped his knuckles with a ruler, he grabbed it from her and whacked her back. Small wonder he left early, after failing to complete his leaving certificate. It's a big wonder they didn't turf him out.

For Harris, it was all about the rugby, and despite eight broken noses, it was a sport he excelled in, winning medals and cups and nurturing an ambition that he might go all the way and wear the green jersey at Lansdowne Road. This sporting life came to a crushing end in 1953 when he contracted TB and was forced into convalescence for two years. He was lucky to survive because tuberculosis remained a significant cause of death in Ireland, with a considerably higher mortality rate than in England at the time.

What he had lost to academia in school, Harris made up for in his sickbed where he directed all his attention to books. A love of drama and a brief dalliance with amateur dramatics informed his move to London in 1954 where the young Harris had been accepted to study acting at the London Academy of Music and Dramatic Art. He had an experience common to many émigrés when he saw a notice in the window of an Earls Court paper shop advertising a room for 30 shillings a week, followed by the message 'No Irishmen or blacks need apply'. He reacted by pulling his sleeve down over his hand, punching through the glass window, removing the offending notice and keeping it as a souvenir.

In the rarefied environs of London theatre, Harris wasn't going to be cast headlong into Shakespearean leads but made his debut when he finagled a part in Brendan Behan's prison drama *The Quare Fellow*. He had overheard someone talking about the production while out drinking one night and decided to make a phone call about it. On being told the part was for a fifty-year-old, Harris explained: 'I look f**king fifty. I haven't had a good meal for four months and I haven't slept in days. Just take a look at me.' They did – and he got the role.

More theatre followed, both in London and Dublin, and the film roles began to trickle in. It's always fun to spot the young Harris among the grizzled tough guys in *The Guns of Navarone* (1961) and as an angry sailor in *Mutiny on the Bounty* (1962). But his knock-out role came in 1963 when Lindsay Anderson chose him for the lead in *This Sporting Life*. As part of the gritty, realistic 'Angry Young Men' films that were starting to emerge from the UK at the time, this was seen as an early classic. Harnessing his hard-nosed Limerick sporting background, Harris played the part of an angry, emotionally stunted, testosterone-fuelled rugby league player from Yorkshire, with Brandoesque style and an accent that's more Limerick than Yorkshire. Widely praised for his authenticity, Harris was nominated for an Oscar and won the award for best actor at the Cannes Film Festival in 1963. I've recently watched it on DVD and it's mind-boggling how good he is. I strongly urge you to go back and catch it if you haven't already.

As a result of all this success, Harris was in serious demand and appeared in dozens of movies, but none of these roles matched the performance that in many ways defined the early part of his career. Maybe some of his potential was wasted away by the already legendary hellraising – who can say? Certainly, any accounts of

Harris's life in the 60s and 70s include words like 'hedonistic' and 'debauched'. Always featuring in lurid tabloid headlines, he dressed in a style that garnered attention and lived in a neo-Gothic mansion in London. He worked hard and played hard, indulging his darker side to his heart's content.

Harris had a particular love of women and they adored the mixture of charm and danger he exuded. 'I overpower women,' he once confessed. He showered them with love and sex and spontaneous partying until he exhausted them, and one woman would never keep his interest for long. His appetite for the next girl, whoever she might be, was insatiable and it's reported that he once flew to New York on Concorde for an afternoon of sex. He picked up and lost two wives along the way, for which he took all the blame: 'I have made seventy movies in my life and been mis-cast twice – as a husband.' Commitment of any kind scared him. It wasn't his thing.

At one point, his cocaine habit got out of control and a stint in hospital saw a priest rushing to Harris's bedside, armed with the last rites. The story goes that Harris woke suddenly to hear the priest reciting the holy rosary and announced to the padre: 'Father, if you are going to hear my confession, prepare to be here for days. By the end of it all, I can guarantee you will very much regret your vow of celibacy.'

At first the film studios accommodated his hellraising, adding extra shooting days to allow for the hangovers and lost weekends, but by the late 70s work was getting thin on the ground. The 'good' life finally caught up with Harris in 1981 when doctors told him he had eighteen months to live if he kept going that way. It was a summer evening when, with typical gusto, he marched into a club for a final drink. He cracked open two bottles of Château Margaux

1957 (£600 per bottle), drank them slowly – he later described the experience: 'I treated them like you'd treat making love to the most gorgeous woman in the world. If you knew you only had one orgasm left, you'd say, "I'm holding it up babe, because I don't want this to end"' – and then stopped taking alcohol. For a decade.

The good roles were still few and far between, though. When he had a shot at playing Maigret in a 1988 TV series, the *Daily Mirror* suggested that his Irish accent made a mockery of the programme, and ironically suggested Harris should go the whole distance: 'How about Sherlock O'Holmes, Paddy Mason, Hercule Guinness?' But this kind of ridicule failed to faze Harris who was well used to the stereotyping that suited elements of the British press. He acquired the rights to the stage production of *Camelot* and took it on a world tour, making a lot of money in the process, and in 1990 he won the London *Evening Standard* Award for best actor for his role as Henry IV.

But perhaps it was a sweet irony that Richard Harris had to come home to put in what many consider to be his finest acting moment – in *The Field* as the megalomaniac farmer Bull McCabe, whose lust for land was visible in the actor's every fibre. Harris was trying on hats for the part when he saw the name of Ray McAnally inside one of them and realized that the great Irish actor had been earmarked for the role before he died. 'I'm very sorry Ray McAnally died,' Harris reportedly commented before adding, 'But I always knew I was destined to play this part.'

Whether it was fate or luck, Harris was right and the part gave him the opportunity for a glorious final lap. Nominated for his second Oscar, Harris was back to his old self when explaining why he didn't want to attend the Oscar ceremony: 'Why the f**k would I want to participate in any of this Hollywood b*****ks. It's fourteen f***ing hours there, fourteen f***ing hours back, two hours of f***ing stupidity and kissing people's f***ing cheeks. F**k that.' . . . It seems he didn't want to go. However, Richard Harris was back in the game and had rediscovered his acting groove. The 90s proved fertile ground for the once-again sought-after actor – even though he'd started back on the Guinness. Close to his seventieth year, Harris moved into a suite at London's Savoy Hotel where he justified the princely rent of £6,000 a week by saying: 'If you're paying the mortgage on a home, you can't ask the bank manager to fetch you a pint.'

Now he was of a certain vintage, the parts offered and taken were appropriate and commanding. And so when Ridley Scott needed an imperial Marcus Aurelius, he went to Harris (*Gladiator*, 2000). When the time came to find Harry Potter's genial headmaster at Hogwarts, it was Harris they called (of which more anon). Producers and film insurance executives notwithstanding, he still enjoyed the occasional night on the lash. He once dragged Alan Rickman and Kenneth Branagh out until four in the morning and, according to Rickman, they had a ball: 'Richard was regaling us with stories about his life, we just sat there with our mouths wide open.'

Harris was without doubt one of the finest actors of the second half of the twentieth century, a fully fledged, high-octane, booze-soaked (for the most part) Irishman who brought a swagger to the silver screen that until then had been lacking. Would he have won more acclaim if he'd curbed what he termed his 'excessive-compulsive' nature? Did he care? Prosaic in his analysis of the acting world, Harris commented shortly before he died: 'Actors take themselves so seriously. Samuel Beckett is important, James Joyce is – they left something behind them. But even Laurence Olivier is totally unimportant. Acting is actually very simple, but actors try to elevate it to an art.' All the same, I contest that British theatre and film would have been far poorer without him. He was what they call a dangerous actor, one who brought colour, unpredictability and emotional integrity to his every role and raised the bar high for all the compatriots who would follow (as well as setting a vertiginous standard for hellraisers).

Harris may have made his home in London and bought a house in the Bahamas, but he remained a proud Irishman, Munster man and Limerick man to the end. When Munster was playing rugby, you'd often find him cheering from the stand, and he was a regular visitor to his family back in the old country. After his death in 2002, a funeral mass was held in his London home but the coffin was draped in the Irish flag. In a final flourish, his ashes were scattered in the exotic surroundings of his Bahamas home and it is there that he swirls mischievously in the Caribbean air today.

PETER O'TOOLE: the Celtic dynamo
Born 2 August 1932

> God, you can love it! But you can't live in it. Oh, the Irish know despair, by God they do. They are Dostoyevskian about it. 'Forgive me Father, I have f**ked Mrs Rafferty.' 'Ten Hail Marys, son.' 'But Father, I didn't enjoy f**king Mrs Rafferty.' 'Good son, good.'

Peter O'Toole is less Irish than Richard Harris in many respects because Harris lived in Ireland till adulthood whereas O'Toole was only a boy when the family emigrated to the UK. But although he had an English accent and took British roles, he always played the

Irish card – and when it came to hellraising he was destined to be the last man standing.

O'Toole's father moved the family from a ruggedly desolate part of Connemara to a Leeds working-class housing estate – what O'Toole later called 'a Mick community' – in search of a better and brighter future. Full of Irish ex-pats and hard-nosed working men, as streets go these were meaner than average. Three of his childhood friends would later be hanged for murder. This was no gilded cage and yet a cursory look at the O'Toole parents gives us some insight into what was to come. Dad, Patrick Joseph O'Toole, was an illegal gambler with a fondness for alcohol and Mum, Connie, loved literature and read stories to young Peter when he was a boy. And so, hailing from Ireland's wild west, reared in a tough part of town in a home that mixed literature and booze with a whiff of rebellion, the foundation stone of the house that Peter would build was laid very early on.

Not unlike Richard Harris, the man who would ride shotgun with him later in life, O'Toole was a poorly child, afflicted as he was with TB, a stammer and poor eyesight. And during his school days he felt the wrath of religious rigour, with nuns who tried to beat him out of left-handedness. O'Toole dedicated a corner of his autobiography to the women in black who tormented him as a youngster, describing the day they went for him after he drew a picture of a horse urinating: 'Flapping, frantic as startled crows, rattling beads and crucifixes, black hooded heads, black winged sleeves, white celluloid breasts, hard, white bony hands banging, the brides of Christ got very cross indeed.' Sounding more and more like Alex or one of his droogs in *A Clockwork Orange*, he continues: 'They tore up my drawing and began to hit me. This made me more cross than those sexless bits of umbrella could ever be so I joined the dance and hit and tore. 'Tis only a gee-gee having a wee-wee you cruel, mad old ruins.'

Later in life, when he criticized the Catholic Church in general and his Catholic upbringing in particular in an interview in *Playboy* magazine, O'Toole was surprised to receive a sackful of post from angry priests and nuns: 'They were shocked. I wrote back saying *I* was shocked – what were they doing reading *Playboy*?'

But back to his younger, less sinful days: O'Toole left school early and earned a crust by packing cartons at a local warehouse before landing a job at the *Yorkshire Evening News*, his local paper, where he went from tea-boy to journalist to bored wannabe: 'I soon found out that, rather than chronicling an event, I wanted to *be* the event.'

Abandoning journalism, he looked to drama as a potential path before being grabbed from his nascent career by a stint of National Service that saw him joining the Royal Navy as a signals operator. This unlikely nautical adventure was followed by a further bid for theatrical glory. Aiming for the top, O'Toole tried his hand at the Royal Academy of Dramatic Art (RADA) but was refused entry on the basis of his academic shortcomings. The flighty would-be actor blew his top and the tirade was fortuitously overheard by RADA principal Sir Kenneth Barnes, who set up an audition that O'Toole passed, resulting in a place at one of the world's foremost theatre schools. It wasn't long before the lithe Irishman was treading the boards and propping up bar counters around London.

O'Toole's acting career was firmly launched in 1959 when he starred in the play *The Long and the Short and the Tall* by Willis Hall, directed by Lindsay Anderson (the same director who had launched Harris, soon to be O'Toole's drinking buddy). His understudy was one Michael Caine, who quickly came to realize that the worst part of being Peter O'Toole's understudy was wondering whether the star would return from the pub before the curtain rose. Night after night, O'Toole kept Caine waiting until the last minute before cantering past and straight on to the stage. Young Caine was charged with sourcing parties, alcohol and women, tasks that drove the beleaguered understudy to comment: 'I'd have made a wonderful pimp.'

There's always a delicious irony to the idea of an Irishman taking on the role of a British national treasure and so it is entirely appropriate for me to dwell on one of British cinema's twentieth-century masterpieces, *Lawrence of Arabia*. The lead role in this gargantuan 1962 production was originally to be played by Marlon Brando, then Albert Finney, but ultimately it came to Peter O'Toole. And by the end of filming, O'Toole was giving Lawrence a run for his money when it came to exploits in the Middle East.

Egyptian film star Omar Sharif became a close friend, a man with whom he had way too much fun in Beirut's hot spots. Asked by a journalist if that entailed getting up to no good, O'Toole replied with a grin: 'Oh darling, do you consider it to be no good? We considered it to be very good indeed.' Among the less salubrious exploits was the night he threw a glass of champagne in a local official's face, leading co-star Alec Guinness to comment 'O'Toole could have been killed, shot or strangled and I'm beginning to think it's a pity he wasn't.'

The film involved a gruelling and physically brutal schedule but the results were worth it. Seriously. I watched it recently and thought it was pretty trippy. Back in 1962, they knew a star was born and O'Toole lapped it up. 'I woke up one morning to find I was famous,' he remarked. 'I bought a Rolls-Royce and drove down Sunset Boulevard, wearing dark specs and a white suit, waving like the queen mum. Nobody took any f**king notice, but I thoroughly enjoyed it.'

And yet, the world did notice Peter O'Toole. It was hard not to. Always wearing his trademark green socks, O'Toole played up his Irishness and floated around town, drinking lavishly and followed by wisps of Gauloise cigarettes that he smoked in an ostentatious cigarette holder. Described by a friend as smelling 'like a French train', Peter was a committed smoker. When John Goodman, his co-star on *King Ralph* (1991), offered to get him an ashtray after he flicked his ash on the ground, he cried, 'Make the world your ashtray, my boy.'

This was the stuff of O'Toole legend: a half-sozzled, licentious thespian with swagger and a talent to back up all the talk. As part of a set of working-class boys who made good, O'Toole, Harris and Richard Burton became their own West End rat pack, lascivious lounge lizards who took the art of candle burning to new levels. Looking back on those days, O'Toole is unapologetic: 'I do not regret one drop. We weren't solitary, boring drinkers, sipping vodka alone in a room. No, no, no: we went out on the town, baby, and we did our drinking in public! . . . It was a fuel for various adventures.' Such fuel allegedly saw him go for a drink in Paris one evening only to wake up in Corsica.

The fuel would come in handy on one of his visits home to Ireland. There was the time O'Toole stayed with his old friend, the movie director John Huston, at his estate in the Wicklow Mountains. The two boys had had a long night of it when we join the story as recounted by O'Toole:

> Came the morning, there was John in a green kimono
> with a bottle of tequila and two shot glasses. He said:

'Pete, this is a day for gettin' drunk!' We finished up on horses, he in his green kimono, me in my nightie in the pissing rain, carrying rifles, rough-shooting it – but with a shih-tzu dog and an Irish wolfhound, who are of course incapable of doing anything. And John eventually came off the horse and broke his leg! And I was accused by his wife of corrupting him!

As with Harris, the booze was blamed for damaging his health. There was a serious illness in 1976, when he required major surgery to remove his pancreas and part of his stomach; then he nearly died in 1978 after succumbing to a severe blood disorder. The booze certainly helped to destroy his marriage to Welsh actress Siân Phillips, from whom he was divorced in 1979. He later said he had studied women for a very long time, had given it his best try, but still he knew 'nothing'.

O'Toole returned to work after his brushes with death but his 1980 Macbeth at the Old Vic made headlines for all the wrong reasons: 'He delivers every line with a monotonous tenor bark as if addressing an audience of deaf Eskimos,' wrote Michael Billington in the *Guardian*. The morning after the disastrous premiere O'Toole opened the door to journalists seeking his reaction and gamely laughed it off – 'It's just a bloody play, darlings!' – but it must have rankled. Later he won his fair share of theatre awards, including a lifetime achievement Olivier Award, but dismissed them as 'trinkets'.

By his seventy-first year, his film work had earned him seven Oscar nominations – two of them for the same character (he played Henry II in both *Becket* (1964) and *The Lion in Winter* (1968)) but none of those shiny statuettes. The Academy attempted to bestow an honorary award but O'Toole initially turned it down, telling the bewildered committee that he was 'still in the game and might win the lovely bugger outright' before urging them to 'please defer the honour until I am eighty'. The Academy (and his daughters) convinced the contrary actor to change his mind and, despite his upset at the lack of booze at the event (apart from the vodka he managed to have smuggled in), Peter O'Toole took to the stage to accept the 'lovely bugger' in 2003.

As if to prove a point, he powered his way to the acting frontline once more when he was nominated for yet another Oscar following a classy performance as an ageing Casanova in the 2006 film *Venus*. It was as if he wanted to score a goal in extra time and, despite not winning the award, O'Toole proved he was still very much in the running. When he retired in 2012, saying, 'The heart of it has gone out of me', he was bowing out more or less at the top of his game.

Despite playing all those English establishment figures, he always remained an Irishman to the core, with a house in Galway as well as one in London. He played cricket for County Galway and often went to Five Nations rugby matches with the two Richards, Harris and Burton. There is a special place in any Irishman's heart for watching England being defeated at rugby. We're at one with the Scots and the Welsh on this. There's a Celtic brotherhood of freedom-fighting, feisty people who have been oppressed by the English. So for the Irish, it's sweet to win at Murrayfield and the Millennium Stadium but the sweetest victory of all is to decapitate the English rose at Twickenham – as I'm sure Harris and O'Toole would have agreed.

Harris has gone now, Burton went long ago, and O'Toole is the last man standing, bemoaning the fact that his drinking partners have left him alone at the bar, an act he considers 'wretchedly inconsiderate'. But behind the beer goggles, who is the man that theatre critic Kenneth Tynan described as an 'insomniac Celtic dynamo'? We'll probably never know; even his own sister, Patricia, can't figure him out. When she met an actress who was about to star with him, she asked, 'At the end of the picture, will you tell me who my brother is? What goes on in there, in the f**king thing he calls a mind?'

It's a question that may never be adequately answered but whatever it is that goes on in there, it helped produce a flamboyant bon viveur who became a legend in his own lifetime – both for his acting and for his hellraising. They simply don't make 'em like that any more.

JONATHAN RHYS MEYERS: born to be king

Born 27 July 1977

My favourite actors, Peter O'Toole, Richard Harris, Richard Burton, they never fulfilled their potential. You'd see absolute brilliance, but they burned the candle at both ends . . . If you want to be in for the long haul, you have to be up to it. You can't go out all night chasing girls and partying.

Hellraisers often fall into one of two categories. One kind tends to pursue the path of boldness, enjoying the notoriety and basking in the anti-glory that ensues. The other type is inclined to fall into the hell that gets raised. This species of hellraiser is more an accidental tourist to a land they didn't particularly want to visit. It is into this latter category that Jonathan Rhys Meyers finds himself, more out of accident than design. A fine actor with a stormy relationship when it comes to booze, Jonathan is well aware of the moniker that has followed him around since he first hit the headlines for less than appetizing reasons. But rather than relishing the hellraiser label, like his predecessors Harris and O'Toole, he has battled it. If you want a career in the film industry today you have to clean up your act so they can get insurance cover for you. It's all about the money. I'm in two minds whether that's a good thing or a bad thing because our hellraisers tend to add to the gaiety of the nation. They're more fun. I personally prefer a bit of roughness round the edges.

Colin Farrell looked set to inherit the hellraiser mantle for a while, with a sex tape, a taste for hard liquor and a long line of model/actress girlfriends, but he managed to go through the mill and come out the other side. I've met him several times and can confirm that he's clean as a whistle, as well as being an extremely affable, articulate and witty guy. We talked about his relationship with the late Elizabeth Taylor in the years before her death – she got him to read a Gerard Manley Hopkins poem at her funeral, where he was one of the only people there who was not a family member. He's sober now but he's still got that naughty glint in his eye and I think that must have been what attracted the woman whose great love was Richard Burton, one of the most infamous hellraisers of all time.

As to why men like Jonathan Rhys Meyers, Colin Farrell and those who blazed a trail of destruction and staggering acting ability before them end up as tabloid headlines, the best place to look is at the beginning of their stories. For Meyers, it was in Dublin city that a premature baby named Jonathan Michael Francis O'Keefe was born and kept in hospital for seven months before being allowed to go home to his mother, Geraldine, on Valentine's Day 1978. Within three years, the family had moved to Cork and Jonathan's parents had separated. Abandoned by his father, he stayed with his mother in a council flat. Unhappy at school, Jonathan Rhys Meyers abandoned education – or, rather, education abandoned him when he was expelled at fifteen years old for truancy. His story around this time is one of poverty and neglect. Geraldine O'Keefe had a serious drink problem and whatever money came in from the state swiftly found a home in the local pub: 'She drank her dole money all the time. The reason she had no money was that she was going out with a lot of other women who had no money, and you start buying drinks all round and it's gone. So you have a lot of friends on Thursday when you have money, and it's all happy. And Friday morning you wake up and have nothing.'

With little else to do, Jonathan headed for the local pool hall and it was there his life changed dramatically in every sense of the word as casting agents happened upon the sultry-looking young man with movie star looks and an attitude to match. An audition followed, he met a director, and within months he was starring in a commercial for Knorr, got paid £500 and thought: 'What boy is not going to say, "I'll do this"? I wanted to act because it was soft money.' Soon afterwards, and by now a fully fledged aspiring actor, Jonathan arrived on the set of Neil Jordan's biopic *Michael Collins* (1996), in which he played the assassin of the Irish revolutionary, and felt very much at home: 'It was just the whole atmosphere, the whole buzz about it, the big cameras and, suddenly, it was kind of like, this is a pretty f**king cool job.'

Success didn't come easily or quickly and Jonathan had to graft to get good parts. Countless auditions were coupled with 'talk' of major parts in films like *Minority Report* and *Spider Man* (and at one point, the next James Bond!), none of which came to pass – but there was good news as the roles started to trickle in. His presence was required and lauded in television projects like *Gormenghast* (2000) and movies that include *Bend it Like Beckham* (2002), *Vanity Fair* (2004), *Matchpoint* (2005) and *Mission: Impossible III* (2006). Jonathan's star was on the rise, but as he has said himself, 'Overnight success takes about ten years.'

A major break came when Jonathan was cast as Elvis in a CBS mini-series (2005). Not only could he transcend the Irish accent and take on a plausible American one but he got the pelvic moves and facial twitches dead on. A Golden Globe quickly followed and the future looked bright. However, within a year, his mother Geraldine died aged just fifty. It was a traumatic time for the young actor and there were stories of dramatic bust-ups with his girlfriend and drinking bouts that ended badly. In a move that distances him from the old-school hellraisers, at the age of just twenty-nine, Jonathan checked into rehab. At the time, he told reporters, 'I am not a hellraiser. I drank for a year and then realised it didn't work for me any more.'

For a while, he replaced the pub with the gym but admitted it was hard to give up drinking, especially when filming in Dublin. He was a man in mourning, in the public eye and in trouble and in some ways there's a deeper tragedy underlying Jonathan's hellraising, one that lacks the sheen of the boozed-up glamour of O'Toole or Harris. Since then there have been a few messy and troublesome scraps in airports and more stints in rehab, but I can tell you that when he came on my show he was slurping nothing more intoxicating than the coffee. He was very calm and a proper gentleman in the Peter O'Toole mould, rather than the tabloid creature that has been created around him. He's got money now but rather than investing in the fancy cars and bling, he's bought himself homes in London, Dublin, Morocco and LA – which all sounds eminently sensible for a poor Irish lad made good.

It should be noted that throughout the whole torrid time, Jonathan was keeping the acting show on the road with arguably his most acclaimed performance to date as Henry VIII in the phenomenally successful mini-series *The Tudors*, a role that won him an Irish Film and Television Academy Award in the Best Actor in a Television Series category, 2008. It's a role that he appeared to relish and one he was more than proud of: 'People have said Henry VIII didn't look like me. Fair enough. But no critic can tell me that how I play Henry isn't right, because I play him a hell of a lot closer to history than people admit. He was an egotistical, spoilt brat, born with the arrogance that everything he had was his by right.'

Meyers was following in the footsteps of Charles Laughton, Richard Burton, Robert Shaw and Keith Michell but he took the role by the scruff of the neck and did it his way – including all the sex scenes, which he said were 'like having sex in a Walmart on a Saturday afternoon'.

Jonathan's own life story couldn't be further removed from that of the most married monarch of them all but you can tell there's plenty more to come from him. Although he's already shown his versatility in going from the King of Rock'n'roll to the King of England, I personally think this actor's best years lie ahead of him if he can keep the demons at bay.

He rejects the hellraiser label, saying: 'I kind of like people having this idea that I'm this wild rebellious guy. But the reality is that I'm not, and I'm not quite sure I want to reveal how boring my life is. Of course, as a young Irish actor you're tarred before you start. It's the enduring cliché.'

What I think he's got in common with the other Irish hellraisers is the ability to play edgy, troubled and explosive characters – perhaps because he's got all that Celtic rage bottled up inside him. Let's park this one for now as 'work in progress'.

*   *   *

It's curious that all three of the hellraisers I've featured here came from difficult backgrounds and fought to achieve their success. They've got an irrepressible, restless spirits and boundless raw talent. Perhaps that self-destruct gene can be channelled into creativity, supplying the high-voltage electrical power that each of them possesses as an actor. Of course, you don't have to have an intense love affair with liquor to be a great actor – there are loads who don't, some of whom I've featured in Chapter 7. But the drinker's unpredictability gives them an edge and makes you feel you don't quite know what they're going to do next – even when they're sober.

2

THE
COMEDIANS

IF YOU WANT TO SEE how much Anglo-Irish attitudes have changed over the last decades, just take a look at the humour. The Bernard Manning era when every paddy was an idiot and 'How many Irishmen does it take to change a lightbulb?' jokes were ten-a-penny have long gone. It would be like doing a joke about a Pakistani or a black woman or a gay man: it's not only politically incorrect but can be illegal and every right-thinking person considers them bad taste. Of course, in Ireland we're allowed our own self-deprecating humour but it's got to be on our own terms. We'll crack a joke about ourselves and call ourselves paddies – but the British are not allowed the paddywhackery now, and some Irish people even got a bit hot under the collar in the 1970s when Dave Allen dipped into it.

Perhaps it's because it's not too long ago that the Irish were seen as *Punch* magazine cartoon images: the potato-eating famine refugee, the drunk navvy or the balaclava-clad terrorist. As recently as the 1980s and maybe the early 90s these were the stereotypes propagated, particularly in right-wing elements of the media. Every Irish comedian who came over to Britain from 1967 to 1997 had to drop in a few gags about terrorism just to get it out of the way because otherwise it was the elephant in the room. But the peace process changed everything, virtually overnight. It changed the acceptability of being Irish in Britain, it changed the nature of comedy and it changed the portrayal of Ireland in the media. Neil Jordan's 1992 (pre-peace-process) film *The Crying Game* was revolutionary enough for showing an IRA man falling in love with what he thought was the girlfriend of a British soldier. But now in 2013 we see Gillian Anderson in *The Fall*, which is about a psychopath running around Belfast killing women and there's not an ArmaLite or a terrorist cell in sight. It's a huge cultural, political, historical shift in the right direction.

By the beginning of the twenty-first century, comedians had torn up their jokes about terrorists, drunken builders and women with twenty-five children. All that is a clichéd bore. We don't laugh at Irishness any more; we laugh at what's genuinely funny – and that's what's made it possible for us to enjoy the ironic post-peace-process sitcom *Father Ted*. Maybe in the past we would have been a bit more sensitive about the three priests banished to Craggy Island for their misdemeanours but now it's just pure comedy and we're all laughing together.

It's not that the Irish are po-faced when it comes to humour. On the contrary, we use it to end an argument, to alleviate sadness or to poke fun at ourselves, but all self-references must be on our terms. And if there's one thing that's always been fertile territory for Irish humour, it's having a dig at authority. As a people we're instinctively, unfailingly anti-authoritarian, probably because of all those centuries of resisting British authority. It's bred into us from an early age; it's in the water. The first comedian I'm going to talk about in this chapter is the one who first made his name for attacking the biggest authority of the twentieth century: our very own Catholic Church (those of a sensitive disposition may want to make the sign of the cross before reading on).

DAVE ALLEN: the funniest man in the pub
6 July 1936–10 March 2005

> I'm bothered by power. People, whoever they might be, whether it's the government, or the policeman in the uniform, or the man on the door – they still irk me a bit. From school, from the first nun that belted me . . .

I remember as a young boy, pyjamas on, sitting on the couch beside my dad and watching him as he chuckled while watching a man on the television. The man was roughly my dad's age (ancient) and appeared to be drinking a whiskey with one hand, occasionally smoking and repeatedly removing non-existent lint from his trousers. It was Catholic Ireland so when this mild-mannered man dressed up as a bishop and started doing fart jokes, I realized we were witnessing a bold man – a very funny, bold man.

The comedy that struck a chord in our house when I was growing up ranged from *The Muppet Show* through to Tommy Cooper via Dermot Morgan and Basil Fawlty and on to Dave Allen. As a family, we appeared to enjoy anarchic yet droll humour that was rarely vulgar but always clever with a twist of mischief. Dave Allen embodied all of these traits. It was dad humour. Everyone's dad loved him. He was that intriguing paradox of being gentle but cutting, intelligent but accessible. You didn't need a degree to get his jokes – just an ability to share his observations.

Allen was born in Dublin and his dad, Cullen, was a journalist and celebrated raconteur who often shared a bar counter with Irish novelist and wit Brian O'Nolan (aka Flann O'Brien aka Myles na gCopaleen). His mum, Jean, was a nurse who happened to be born in England. With a story-telling father and an English mother, it's perhaps no wonder Dave Allen ended up sitting on a stool on British TV telling funny stories for a living.

His Irish background would very much inform his future career and the substance of his routines, so many of which revolved around the Catholic Church and a questioning irreverence towards that institution and all who sailed in her. He was a pupil at Beaumont convent school, which was run by nuns whom he described as 'the Gestapo in drag'. Unhappy as he might have been at the time, these nuns would go on to inform much of Allen's later comedy: 'I arrived at this convent, with these Loreto nuns, and the first thing that was said to me was: "You'll be a *good* boy, won't you?" And I went: "What?" So they said: "When you come in here, you'll be a *good* boy, because bold and bad and naughty boys are punished!" And I'd never seen a crucifix before. All I could see was this fella nailed to a cross! I thought: "Shit! I *will* be good!"'

He went on to Terenure College in Dublin, another Catholic school which, he recalled, combined cruel corporate punishment with ominous talk of sex and its association with the Devil himself. Somewhat unsurprisingly, Allen was expelled and left school altogether at the age of sixteen. A few journalistic jobs followed (clerk at the *Irish Independent*, writer with the *Drogheda Argus*) before he decided to try his luck in London, having run out of options at home. His attempts to get a job on Fleet Street came to nothing but he was more successful at Butlin's, where he got his first taste of audience approval as a Redcoat. Sitting telling jokes and stories between the evening's acts suited him right down to the ground and he decided to focus on comedy full-time. First he changed his name from the alien linguistic mouthful David Edward Tynan O'Mahony to the less complicated Dave Allen (a stage name that cannily secured alphabetical top-billing). He was still Irish – just not quite so much.

It was the early days of television and Allen seized the opportunity when he appeared on the BBC talent show *New Faces*. He toured with the singer Helen Shapiro and by 1963, he was joined in the support-act dressing room by up an unstoppable force of nature called The Beatles. It was in Australia where he got his biggest break when he hosted *Tonight with Dave Allen* – a show that ran for eighty-four episodes. (In an odd romantic twist I can't resist mentioning, Allen was linked to the feline singer Eartha Kitt who appeared on the weekly show twice. The pair were seen holding hands in public but nothing was to come of it and the story died. Shame, really.)

Back in the UK in 1964, with an Australian wife in tow instead of an American sex kitten, Allen built up a reputation as host of *Sunday Night at the Palladium* and as resident comedian on a show hosted by another Irishman abroad, Val Doonican (see Chapter 8). By 1967, he was established enough to go it alone when he started hosting *Tonight with Dave Allen* on ITV and it was here that the character we all came to know and admire emerged with barstool, half-smoked cigarette and a glass of what we all presumed was whiskey. The drinking and smoking put you at your ease. You felt you could sit there and have a dialogue with him. He's like the funniest man in the pub. Now, of course, the funniest man in the pub can sometimes be the funniest man in the pub and he can sometimes be the pub bore, but Allen really *was* the funniest man in the pub and you wanted to sit there and listen to his stories all night, perhaps with a glass of your own in hand.

A mixture of monologues and sketches made the BBC take notice and it was on this channel that *The Dave Allen Show* and *Dave Allen at Large* dominated the comic airwaves between 1968 and 1979. Allen's experience of a Catholic education and life in a near-theocratic society informed his material, and sex and the demonization of it by the Church loomed large too. The confession box was a regular target. Allen described it as akin to 'talking to God's middle-man, a ninety-five-year-old bigot'. Back home in Ireland, though, few in authority saw the funny side of Dave Allen's jokes and in 1977 his shows were banned on RTÉ. The Church was still a very big noise at the time, and perhaps viewers were writing in saying 'Get this filth off the air!' But it did him no harm to be banned in his home country; it all helped to build the anti-authoritarian image we know and love.

As Allen's star ascended in London and beyond, there were typically Irish rumblings emerging from the auld sod where he was being chastised for mocking Irish people in his routine. Reporting on an awkward-sounding encounter with the comedian, writer (then *Irish Times* journalist) Maeve Binchy wrote:

> Yes, of course he gets attacked by people for sending up the Irish, oh certainly people have said that there's something Uncle Tom-like about his sense of humour, an Irishman in Britain making money by laughing at Irishmen, but he gets roughly the same amount of abuse for laughing at black people, at Jews, at the Tory Party, at the Labour Party, at the Pope, at vicars. People become much more incensed if he makes fun of someone else's minority group than their own, he thinks.

The point was that the Irish didn't want to feel the British were being given ammunition with which to mock them; the patronizing attitudes during those centuries of hurt were still too keenly felt.

It was in the mid-70s that Allen's irreverence became a national talking point. Dressed as the Pope, the comedian pretended to do a striptease on the steps of the Vatican to the tune of 'The Stripper'. Protests followed, with letters and calls to the BBC complaining about the disrespectful scene. And the complaints, as so often can be the way, were the making of him. Allen returned to Australia to film four shows for which he was paid AUS$100,000 and when he got back to England, he sold out in theatres across the land. It wasn't just the Church that bore the brunt of his humour: he took a dim view of politicians, and Protestant Northern Irishman Ian Paisley was a frequent target. Anyone in any kind of authority was fair game.

By the 1980s, Dave Allen's casual story-telling technique and some of his reference points were seen as out-dated by a new set of brash, fast-talking, so-called alternative comedians whose style pretty much reflected the era. It was the shouty political comedy of Ben Elton, Alexei Sayle and Ade Edmondson audiences wanted to watch – for a while at least. Allen announced his official retirement but staged a brief comeback on the BBC in 1990 and on ITV in 1993 that led him to explain: 'I'm still retired, but in order to keep myself in retirement in the manner in which I'm accustomed, I have to work. It's a kind of Irish retirement.'

The comeback was restricted due to poor health but there was time for Allen to lob one more grenade at the establishment when he told his now infamous 'clock' joke: 'We spend our lives on the run. You get up by the clock, you go to work by the clock, you clock in, you clock out, you eat and sleep by the clock, you get up again, you go to work – you do that for forty years of your life and then you retire – what do they f***ing give you? A clock!'

Unbelievably, some 'high-minded' members of the British parliament took the BBC to task for lack of taste because of the use of the F word in the punchline. The Beeb kowtowed but Allen was unapologetic: 'I'm Irish and we use swearing as stress marks.'

Slowly, his career was coming to an end but not before he received belated recognition by the bright young things of British comedy, who wisely awarded Allen the lifetime achievement award at the British Comedy Awards in 1996. Looking back on his career, Allen wondered aloud where his comedy came from and ended up thanking a comic deity for the nuggets that fuelled his career: 'I don't know if there's somebody out there, some god of comedy, dropping out little bits saying, "Here, use that, that's for you, that's to keep you going."' Personally, I think his Irishness was the root of his material; it gave him the anger and anarchy.

The British public heard Dave Allen's last performance on BBC Radio 4 in 1999 before he retired fully and indulged in his favourite hobby, painting. He had already given up the sixty-a-day smoking habit, telling friends: 'I was fed up with paying people to kill me; it would have been cheaper to hire the Jackal to do the job.' But it still caught up with him and he died of emphysema in 2005 while his second wife was pregnant with a son he would never meet (he had two children from a previous marriage).

Towards the end of his life, there was a renewed respect for Dave Allen with comedians like Jack Dee, Pauline McLynn, Ed Byrne and Dylan Moran citing him as a significant influence. On hearing of Allen's death, Eddie Izzard described him as 'a torchbearer for all the excellent Irish comics who have followed in recent years'.

There have been Dave Allen revivals on the telly recently and when I watch them I can see exactly what my dad saw in him in the 1970s. It's observational comedy that hits a nerve, that makes you go 'Yeah, I agree, I'm right with you there.' It's surprising how little has dated, even in these days when the Church doesn't have such a fierce hold on our souls. I'd like to take this opportunity to say to Dave Allen what he always said to us at the end of his shows: 'Goodnight, thank you, and may your god go with you.'

DYLAN MORAN: telling it like it is
Born 3 November 1971

Real life is fine. But you can only take so much of it.

Like Dave Allen's, Dylan Moran's stage persona enjoys a drink and he slurs and staggers as if he's already had a couple of sharpeners: 'A comedy club always seemed to me the extension of a pub so there's no reason not to have a drink in your hand.' The character he creates is like the embarrassing drunk at a social gathering saying the stuff that everyone else is thinking but is too polite to say. It's a very Irish thing, according to Moran: the congenital drunk in the corner of the Irish pub will suddenly burst out 'You're all talking shite and I'm going to tell you why. For the next hour.'

In his stage show, he has some great 'telling it like it is' skits:

You know when you're late and you arrive and say 'I'm so sorry. Traffic. Traffic was terrible. And there was a fire as well. A small boy – I had to give him an eye operation and all I had was a spatula and a banana.' You should just tell the truth. You should just walk in and say 'I knew you were here. I knew you were waiting. I was at home and do you know what I did? I had a bun. And it was delicious. Because I knew you were waiting. I'll have a glass of wine – thank you very much.'

Moran says it all goes back to when he was young and 'there were old relatives who would tell me stories and they might be funny or they might bore the arse off me'. He grew up in Navan, County Meath with a carpenter father and a mother who wrote poetry and taught him the importance of words from the word go. Like Dave Allen and Peter O'Toole before him, Moran raged against his religious education; he was 'depressed by the priestly omnipresence' and all the people telling him 'stop it, don't, put it down, sit down, be quiet'. He left school at the age of sixteen and drifted around for a few years, writing poetry and briefly, incongruously, working in a florist's before, at the age of twenty, he ended up in Dublin's Comedy Cellar – a small club above a bar – and caught the bug.

The act he developed was a meandering stream of consciousness – like Dave Allen, he's the funniest man in the pub when it's working well, but he's much weirder than Allen. The oddness was also captured in a column he wrote for the *Irish Times* on random topics – recipes, insects, you name it; he'd take any subject and float off with it. After a couple of years doing the clubs in Dublin, he came across the water: 'I had to make some money. I had to earn a living. So I thought "I've been having a great time playing with mud pies, but will anybody buy them?" And that's why I went to London.'

He found it hard at first; the comedy circuit can be a thankless slog and he might not have continued if he hadn't won the 'So

You Think You're Funny' competition at the Edinburgh Festival in 1993, followed by the coveted Perrier Award in 1996. After that it all started to happen for him and he got a role in a BBC Two sitcom *How Do You Want Me*, then co-wrote *Black Books* with fellow Irishman Graham Linehan (of whom more later). Bernard Black, the character he created and played in *Black Books*, is a droll, put-upon bookshop owner who's not interested in much apart from smoking, drinking and reading – and somehow you get the impression he's not much different from Moran himself.

According to Moran, there are differences between comedy in England and Ireland. In England, 'you are the man who has a licence to say anything, which acts as an icebreaker for everyone in the room'. That's not needed in Ireland where we're used to our outspoken characters and the ice rarely needs breaking. Maybe that's why Moran has been more successful in the UK than back at home. He relishes the fact that he's seen as an eccentric. 'In Ireland there's great tolerance of "the character". People say "Ah, don't mind Jimmy – he always wears a bag on his head." And in England these people are anathema, they're pariahs, you cross to the other side of the street because they get in the way of your day and fuck it up.' He's happy to be the pariah, the one expressing himself in his own unique way. It gives him his edge.

Moran says it's not the material that makes his act work, though: it's about timing: 'I understood there was a certain tension needed to make people laugh, so I created tension and built it to a point at which they laughed.' He doesn't tell jokes – he just opens his mouth and off he goes. On occasion he has bombed when the audience just didn't get that stream-of-consciousness thing or his timing was off, and nowadays he's focusing more on the TV work but still does comedy festivals worldwide. He's settled in Edinburgh, with a wife and two children, but looks back nostalgically at the old days in Dublin when he was starting out: 'The most fun I had, the most pleasure, was in the early Comedy Cellar days. And what matters to me is being able to still walk into the Cellar and make people laugh.'

FATHER TED: Irish lunacy

21 April 1995–1 May 1998

The show's ... not about paddywackery clichés. It's essentially a cartoon. It's demented. It has its own world and as much integrity as *The Simpsons*.

– Dermot Morgan

There was a time when mockery of the Church in Ireland was an offence deemed strong enough for placard-wielders to stand outside a cinema or theatre decrying the contents of the offending film or play (one they had likely not seen). *The Life of Brian* was banned in Ireland for donkey's years and, more recently, the placards were out for *The Last Temptation of Christ*. In fact, where I work in RTÉ, the men and women of the placard have been busy throughout 2013 in all weathers decrying the presence of too much sex on our television screens. It's a democracy, they are perfectly entitled to their placards and opinions; in fact, I quite admire their passion. At least they're standing for something. In *Father Ted*, there is a famous scene that sees protestors waving signs, among them one that says 'DOWN WITH THIS SORT OF THING'. It's odd then that when *Father Ted* appeared on Irish television in 1995, there wasn't a placard to be seen. What happened?

It seems Irish comedy had come full circle from Dave Allen. When the sitcom about the three priests living with their housekeeper on Craggy Island first screened, most people didn't particularly care that the Church was being mocked; not a question was raised about it. Twenty years earlier it simply wouldn't have been countenanced, but attitudes to the Catholic Church had changed. First of all there were the stories about priests who had secretly had children, then it moved into deeper and more terrible waters with the news that some priests had been abusing children, so I suspect the powers that be felt they weren't in a strong position to criticize. Unfettered by protest, one of the funniest sitcoms of the twentieth century came on screen to wide praise and much applause. Essentially, *Father Ted* did for the priesthood what *Fawlty Towers* did for the hotel business – made us not take it too seriously.

It all started when Irish writers Graham Linehan and Arthur Mathews got together to brainstorm some ideas for comic sketches and characters. Both had form: between them, they had worked on *Alas Smith and Jones* and *The Fast Show* as well as writing material for Alexei Sayle and Harry Enfield. They came up with the idea for a comic documentary with each episode focusing on a particular Irish 'type' and the first episode featured a scheming but loveable goon called Father Ted. They pitched it to Hat Trick Productions and Channel 4 in the UK, and the response was that they didn't want the mockumentary but they'd love to see a sitcom about Father Ted.

Off the boys went and dreamed up the idea for the show we all know and love. Three priests have been sent to Craggy Island in penance for past misdemeanours and they live there with their housekeeper, Mrs Doyle, who keeps trying to give them cups of tea and trays of sandwiches. The storylines tend to involve Father Ted getting himself into embarrassing scrapes then digging ever-deeper holes as he attempts to lie and cheat his way out of them. The script was good but it needed exactly the right cast to make it work. Fortunately, they already knew who they wanted in the lead role . . .

For Irish readers of my generation, 80s television comedy was defined and exemplified by one man: stand-up mimic and actor Dermot Morgan was a staple on RTÉ television. Our parents roared laughing at him throughout the decade of Thatcher and Haughey while just a few years later, nerdy students like myself sat by the radio to hear him on *Scrap Saturday*, Irish radio's version of Britain's *Spitting Image* (a show we could and did watch in Ireland too). Morgan had a way with voices and he hooked up with quality scriptwriters to sharpen the wit. The show poked fun at the great and the good to the point that it disappeared mysteriously one Saturday morning, never to be seen again. Morgan was gutted and called the decision to axe it 'a shameless act of broadcasting cowardice and political subservience'. I was gutted too. It had mercilessly lampooned our political leaders and public figures in a way that's very important in a democracy and nothing immediately stepped into the breach.

Morgan slogged long and hard on the comedy circuit in Ireland where one of his characters, Father Trendy, a 'cool' and 'with it' priest, remained a constant favourite. That's why, when the producers of *Father Ted* called in 1994, he was more than ready for the challenge and stepped into the lead role with aplomb.

Father Dougal, the bumbling priest who is not overburdened with brains, was played by Ardal O'Hanlon, while the role of Father Jack, the potty-mouthed alcoholic, went to Frank Kelly. My favourite character, Mrs Doyle, was played by Pauline McLynn with such exceptional comic finesse that her catchphrases were soon in use nationwide.

'Will you have a cup of tea?'

'No thanks, Mrs Doyle.'

'Ah, go on go on go on go on go on go on go on go on go on go on . . .'

'I won't have a cup right now.'

'You will you will you will you will you will you will you will you will you will . . .'

She's every Irish mother of a certain vintage, constantly bringing in trays full of sandwiches that no one is ever going to eat, and I love her.

Top actors and comics queued up to be part of the joke: Graham Norton played the high-camp Father Noel Furlong in three episodes and Ed Byrne played a teenager mocking Father Ted on a telephone chatline. The show had that buzz right from the start and everyone involved knew it was going to be big. The first series quickly acquired cult status when it was broadcast on Channel 4 and it is still pretty much shown on a loop on RTÉ 2. Awards followed: in 1998 *Father Ted* got a BAFTA for Best Comedy, Dermot Morgan got one for Best Actor and Pauline McLynn got Best Actress.

Two more series were filmed before Morgan announced that he would be leaving the show for fear of being typecast. One night after the final day's filming on the final series, he and his partner, Fiona, were hosting a dinner party in London when he collapsed and died of a heart attack at the age of forty-five. He remains one of the more poignant 'what-ifs' in his contribution to stage and screen on these islands.

The show couldn't go on without Morgan (although an American production company is filming a US remake with priests set on an island off the New England coast). Like *Fawlty Towers*, it would never have time for the jokes to grow tired so will always retain its cult status.

Father Ted is probably the purest fusion of Irish and British comedy. Commissioned by Channel 4, it had an all-Irish cast, spent much time filming in the beautiful County Clare and had Irish writers. We would have complained loudly if the British had written a sitcom about three corrupt, scheming, totally unreligious priests. In the same way as only gay people can call themselves queer and only black people are allowed to use the 'n' word, we are the only ones allowed to mock ourselves in general but priests in particular. And the comedy in *Father Ted* is as Irish as it gets: very funny, very clever and spiritually satirical, with its post-ironic political incorrectness.

DARA O BRIAIN: the most Irish of them all
Born 4 February 1972

This is the first time in my lifetime that Irish people are able to go: 'What? You're going to England? Sure, it's full of terrorists. Come to Ireland. We've no terrorists at all. They're all playwrights now.'

As eras go, the early 90s weren't that bad. Bill Clinton brought rock and roll and blowjobs to the White House. Ireland elected a woman as president and qualified for its first-ever World Cup finals. Nirvana, Blur and The Cranberries burst on to the scene as U2 continued to reinvent and give them all a master class in stamina. As a nerdy student at University College Dublin I found myself moving in varied circles that took in politics, history and the bar. As I did so, I found myself brushing shoulders (mine narrow, his broad) with a most articulate and very amusing science type who emerged as a star of the debating circuit. Holding court in whatever lecture theatre he performed in, Dara O Briain was always going to end up in a job where his voice would be heard.

Brought up in Bray, County Wicklow, the O'Briains spoke Irish at home and Dara attended an Irish-speaking school in a Dublin sub-urb. At University College Dublin, he studied theoretical physics but, between lectures, his head was turned by the banter and repartee that dominated college debating societies. It wasn't long before the motion for discussion became irrelevant as the lecture theatres filled to hear the mile-a-minute science student divert the discussion to suit his observations. Story-telling and quick-witted comebacks were the order of the day rather than stand-alone gags and it was in these student lecture halls that Dara honed his skills and saw the potential of a career in comedy.

The next step was to gain some exposure and earn a few quid on the national broadcaster. A stint on children's television and as a panellist on a satirical panel show was complemented by constant gigging around the world with much time spent in Australia and at festivals like Edinburgh, where his shows were attracting some very important interest.

Most of the subjects in this book simply outgrew Ireland. For a country that prides itself on the ability to talk and talk and talk, sometimes it feels like going around in circles and, for some people, the circles become too small and so a toe is dipped into the Irish Sea. Dara's career went as far as it could in Ireland and he couldn't resist the temptation to look over the hedge at a bigger field: 'You're sitting next door to a country of 60 million people which has Christ knows how many hundreds of comedy clubs and God knows how many hundreds of theatres. This country [UK] is uniquely set up because of the Victorian infrastructure of theatres to be really good for stand-up comedy and they're receptive to it and they have a great tradition of it so it's essentially like playing in the Premier League.'

The road to Britain was smooth with no concerns over potential obstructions like accents. The path had been well trod by Dave Allen, Dylan Moran was on the circuit, and Graham Norton already had his own irreverent chat show (see Chapter 3), so Irish comedians were welcome and not lost in translation. One of the most striking things about Dara O Briain is that, unlike Dave Allen, he didn't invent a new name for himself. Causing difficulty even for a home audience, it's a name few would have predicted would be rolling off the tongues of the British audiences who flock to his shows. And, in fact, back in 2006 Dara explained: 'Darby Brown, Dazzy B, Dusky Benderson . . . Don't think that I don't spend all day running through the incredible showbiz career I might have if I just ditched my own name.' He told me: 'It's easier to become well known with a name like Jack Dee or Alan Carr or Jimmy Carr or Jo Brand. They're all short, punchy names as opposed to some big convoluted thing!' But to his credit, Dara has always done things a little differently.

Things really kicked off in the UK in 2003 when Dara took the helm of *Live Floor Show* on BBC Two. This was followed swiftly by a guest appearance as host of *Have I Got News for You*. After that, everything started to happen and in between countless gigs at venues all over Ireland and the UK, Dara was fronting shows like *Mock the Week* and partaking in popular series such as *Three Men in a Boat*, which saw him reconstruct the famous novel with Griff Rhys Jones and Rory McGrath.

The material he chose for his stage show was quite different from Dave Allen's day. There are very few Church-related gags in Dara's repertoire, although he'll still have a poke at authority figures such as politicians or bankers. The shadow of the Troubles was receding when he got to Britain in the late 1990s: 'We arrived at the point where the worst effect it had on me is the time I couldn't find a bin on the Tube and a bloke said "Oh, that'll be because of your lot."' He learned to do his terrorism joke first, so it was out of the way and the audience relaxed – and also because it was very easy laughs. 'There is a weird notion that terrorism is a difficult thing to write about. It's the f**king easiest thing because the tension is already there so if you address it anyway, you release that tension and you get a laugh. We got credit for a darkness and a depth that we did not deserve.' But now, post-peace process, it's history; there's no comedy in it any more.

The only major consideration for the twenty-first-century Irish comedian is how Irish or how British his material can or shall be. Most comedy can be universal but in Ireland we'll munch a packet of Tayto rather than Walkers crisps, and if you're talking politics most British people don't know how to pronounce Taoiseach, never mind have a clue who the latest one is. Dara gigs in both countries and he'll riff about the same type of subjects but just change the Irishness of the references as appropriate. He's one of life's comedy riffers. You can throw anything at him and he'll riff away, like the perfect jazz guitarist in a band.

Broadly speaking, he's an observational comic, looking at life today. He's not looking at Ireland as a country or playing up being an Irish lad in the UK – even though he's possibly the proudest Irishman of all the émigrés in this book. He was brought up to speak fluent Irish, in a very Irish household, and you can sense the

Irishness in his bones. As a prolific tweeter, he allows his fans (and naysayers) close to him in a technological sense and, on occasion, this has allowed detractors to criticize him if he says anything that they deem un-Irish. Dara reckons 'It is generally a bedroom Republican, it's teenage nationalists going "Ahh, I thought you were Irish." I did find if you transferred the language to Irish, it ends quite quickly.'

It's a good ploy when challenging a critic of one's Irishness to simply 'out-Irish' them with a passing phrase in the mother tongue. But this type of criticism does rankle with Dara, who says, 'I think it's exceptionally rude, particularly in a time of more emigration, to turn around to anyone's that emigrated and say "You're not Irish now." I think it's an immature trait.'

When we met in London for the purposes of this book, we talked at length about the Irish in Britain and Dara said the move wasn't so dramatic for him as it was for generations before him. As he settled into his new home he found that the Irish had assimilated into British society and weren't seen as different any more. 'Cheap flights and access to the country just wiped that out . . . if anything, you have to remind them that you're Irish.'

Up to this point, those who conquered the UK did so while being defined by their Irishness. Dara was the first man for whom it really doesn't matter. He'd be funny if he was Scottish or Dutch or Kazakhstani. However, that doesn't mean that he has forsaken his nationality or sense of loyalty to Ireland. Listening to him talk, I get the sense that he has a recalibrated patriotism that allows him to rule Britannia and honour Hibernia at the same time:

> Because I work so often in Ireland I'm still quite Irish in some ways. [Graham] Norton has assimilated better.

He'll appear in the *Radio Times* in a Union Jack waistcoat to do the *Eurovision*, which I would find uncomfortable, I'd find that weird. I tweet about following Ireland in the football and on *Mock the Week* I still talk about 'your' football team even though, nominally it's 'our' government because I live here and pay my taxes.

I tried him with the critical question: who does he support when he watches the World Cup? As part of his recalibrated patriotism, Dara has no time for those who shout for whomever England happen to be playing against: 'You kind of have to lose that here [in the UK] because it's emotionally perverse to wish ill on your loved ones and friends that they should be unhappy. I don't cheerlead for the English football team but I'm not basking in their misery.'

Always in demand for his brand of what he describes as 'frippery, quippery and off-the-cuffery', Dara is ensconced in Britain as a permanent fixture on television and the comedy circuit. It's been an odd route but he got there. As he said in 1999, 'given my education, I really should be a teacher in Carlow Institute of Technology or somewhere, teaching first years how to differentiate'. Mathematics' loss has been comedy's gain, so it all adds up in the end.

*   *   *

We've got many other stand-up comedians who've crossed the water but the three comics I've covered in this chapter are, for me, the ones who've really raised themselves above the rest – and Allen and O Briain were especially ground-breaking. We've noted the progression over thirty years of comedy from addressing Irishness and seeing the funny side of things like Catholic guilt through to not giving it so much as a passing mention. From feeling a need to lighten the atmosphere by cracking an Irish terrorist joke through to cracking jokes about the terrorism in England. From lightbulb jokes about dumb paddies through to Dara O Briain, who's by far the cleverest man in comedy on either side of the Irish Sea.

One thing the comedians I've chosen have in common (and this is true of most Irish comics) is that their material is not about jokes, it's about telling stories or just talking. In Ireland, one of the things we do better than anyone else is talk. We have a certain flair when it comes to words, a love of vocabulary and quirky turns of phrase. The gift of the gab, the blarney, call it what you will, is one of our national traits. That's why it's hardly surprising we've made a name for themselves in the UK in jobs where chatting is a prerequisite. And that's why the Irish have given the UK quite so many of the household names I'll talk about in the next chapter, "The Chat Show Hosts' . . .

3

THE CHAT SHOW HOSTS

THE MINUTE MICHAEL PARKINSON comes on television you can tell he is a Yorkshireman, while the Davids – Dimbleby and the late Frost – sound a bit posher and more southern, and Jonathan Ross has a working-class geezer accent. The point is that, rightly or wrongly, you think you know straight away whether they are descended from aristocrats or brickies, went to private school or the local comprehensive, and say 'toilet' rather than 'loo'. Conversely, when someone from Ireland comes on television in the UK, the accent is classless. You can't tell how many bedrooms there were in their childhood home or whether their family employed servants or worked below stairs themselves. The fact that we don't fall neatly into the British class system helps the Irish when trying to make it in the UK. It makes us neutral – which is a good thing when our job is to draw other people out. We don't have any chips on the shoulder; we just want to ask questions because we're curious.

The British perceive the chatty Irish chat show host as genial and unthreatening. Guests know they're not going to be Paxmanned over the head or joked into a corner by one too many one-liners. A lot of modern chat shows have the host rat-a-tatting at guests, both here and in the United States (think Leno and Letterman) and the substance of the interview can get lost along the way.

Now, chat shows are a subject I know a bit about. The *Late Late Show* has been on RTÉ in Ireland for fifty-one years, making it the world's longest-running chat show apparently. Gay Byrne presented it for thirty-seven years, Pat Kenny had it for ten, and I took over five years ago. I always say it's not my show – the show is like the Tardis and I'm just the latest Doctor – but I was enormously honoured to be asked. It's a big challenge because it is 100 per cent live every Friday night from half nine through to midnight, and it runs for thirty-eight weeks a year. We have everyone on, from politicians to pop stars, Hollywood royalty to the individuals making headlines in any given week. I always make it my business to go to the dressing room beforehand and look guests in the whites of the eyes so they can see I'm not too scary. Lots of celebrities are nervous because we're live – and I know how they feel because I'm often nervous as well – but you just go out the other side of the curtain and have some fun.

With a show like that back home, why have so many of our chat show hosts crossed the water to grace UK TV screens? Well, the bigger audiences must have been a draw. It must be nice to get 8 million viewers rather than seven hundred thousand. Gay Byrne flirted with it for a while before deciding against a move, but many others have filled prime-time spots on British screens over the last fifty years. Most of them are seen as 'charming', 'non-threatening' and 'affable', words that are quite often associated with the Irish. But the influence of these charming men has gone far beyond a bit of superficial television, as I'll explain with reference to some of our greatest TV exports.

EAMONN ANDREWS: Mr Congeniality

19 December 1922–5 November 1987

> He let people be the stars.
> – Val Doonican

Any broadcaster worth his salt knows that to understand the history of Irish broadcasting you need to acquaint yourself with the granddaddy of them all. Eamonn Andrews is probably the patron saint of Irish television, having been there from the beginning, and then for decades he spun the two plates of Irish and British presenting jobs. He was a monolithic figure who casts a long shadow in this field.

My first memory of him is as a big, good-natured man who clasped a large red book while proclaiming to an unsuspecting victim 'This is your life!' – at which point some dramatic music swirled out of the ether and the credits rolled on a show that was effectively a funeral for someone still alive. I was too young to notice or care that the man had a distinctly Irish accent but he was always considered 'one of ours' and the fact that his surname was the same as my mother's maiden name (although there's no relation) made me pay a bit more notice.

In the modern reception area of Ireland's national broadcaster, RTÉ, there's an impressive bronze statue of the broad-shouldered Andrews, arms folded. He looks authoritative and important and could be fierce if it wasn't for a genial smile on his sculpted face. People pass him by on their way into television studios, mostly ignoring the presence of this broadcasting giant. But his story, that of a working-class boy from Dublin who conquered the British airwaves, is irresistible and too interesting simply to skip by in a hurry.

Andrews's dad was a carpenter with the Electricity Supply Board but also a drama enthusiast, an interest that proved hereditary. A fan of Gary Cooper and Spencer Tracy, young Eamonn Andrews was drawn to the gentle-giant characters of American cinema despite the fact that he was painfully shy as a child; according to his biographer Tom Brennand, 'He was born to blush, to be embarrassed, to be pathologically shy, and he grew up almost too timid to speak to anyone.' In fact, bullying became such a problem for the tall, slightly odd-looking boy at Dublin's Synge Street School that he took up boxing. This was a clever move for two reasons. For starters, he was never bullied again, and secondly, although he didn't realize it at the time, it would help to launch his media career.

A working-class lad, Eamonn attended elocution classes to make him sound less rough around the edges and started to get occasional work as a boxing commentator on Irish radio. His love of boxing and an interest in journalism dovetailed neatly in 1944 when he began commentating on and competing in the amateur boxing championships. The ambitious sportsman jumped straight from the commentator's box into the ring before going on to win his final fight, becoming junior Irish middleweight champion in 1944.

By this time, Andrews was hungry for the limelight and wanted to broaden his horizons. To this end, he started to bombard the BBC. 'A constant stream of letters poured across the Irish Sea from the Andrews household to Broadcasting House,' he recalled. 'Nearly all were answered politely, but all said the same thing – "Sorry, but . . . "' Attempts to catch the attention of BBC bosses proved fruitless until 1950 when he was asked to host *Ignorance is*

Bliss, a comedy quiz on BBC radio. Five years after the end of the Second World War, the Beeb were looking for accents that weren't as plummy as those that had previously characterized the station. Eamonn Andrews epitomized this new 'sound'. They also liked the way he was perceived by listeners (and later viewers): 'He sells an ordinariness. The British public quite like that, they like to think they could do what you can do if they like you.' He was Everyman: a genial Irish Everyman with a broad grin.

His soft Irish brogue accepted, Andrews was told to consider a name-change. Eamonn is a common enough name in Ireland – despite it sounding like a Jamaican greeting – but his agent thought it too Irish and suggested he try 'something reliable and homely, like Bob'. There was already a broadcaster called Bob Andrews so the agent suggested he go the whole hog and change his name to Bob Jones, but Eamonn decided to stick to his guns and stayed true to his real name. It stuck and proved unproblematic for British audiences but not so easy for the occasional American guest like the actor Jon Voight. The *Midnight Cowboy* star was filming a piece for an episode of *This Is Your Life*. When the tape was being tidied up for broadcast, the production team heard Voight saying, 'Hello Eamonn? Eamonn? What the f**k sort of name is Eamonn?'

With the advent of television, Andrews made a seamless transition from radio to the medium that made him one of Britain's most recognized faces. *What's My Line?*, a game show in which contestants were questioned by celebrity panellists to try to find out what their occupations were, ran for twelve years (1951–63) on the BBC in tandem with other television staples such as the children's shows *Playbox* (1955) and *Crackerjack* (1955–64). It was on *Crackerjack* that Andrews had a memorable encounter with the Queen who, when visiting the set, was presented with pens for Charles and Anne and an Andy Pandy doll for her son, young Prince Andrew. Andrews remembered the first two names but forgot the youngest royal . . .

> 'Your Majesty, this is for . . .' he began, then stopped.
> The Queen waited politely.
> 'This is for . . .' he said again, then stopped and began to perspire.
> This time the Queen came to his rescue: 'For the little one, Mr Andrews.'
> 'Yes ma'am,' said a relieved Eamonn. 'This is for the little one.'

The hard work paid off and his bosses took on board his suggestion to make a British version of the hit American television show *This Is Your Life*. 'After my first viewing of *This Is Your Life*, I said to myself "This Is television",' Andrews explained, and he went on to present the show for the BBC between 1955 and 1964. As is so often the way, critics hated the show but 12 million people begged to differ on a weekly basis as they tuned in to watch Andrews, armed with a big red book, a microphone and a fake beard, taking celebrities by surprise before sitting them down to a career retrospective.

In the midst of all this, the arch multi-tasker continued to present programmes on Irish radio and became chairman of a committee that was set up to advise on establishing the Irish television station RTÉ, then became its first chairman. So he never lost his Irish connection. He kept one foot on each side of the Irish Sea.

Andrews was disappointed when BBC bosses decided to drop *This Is Your Life* in 1964, feeling it had lost its novelty, but he moved to ITV with a Sunday night chat show that lasted five years and then resurrected his signature show. The Thames run of *This Is Your Life* lasted from 1969 until 1987, thus becoming one of the longest-running programmes ever aired on British television, and it brought Andrews into the homes of millions of British viewers every week, trailing only *The Benny Hill Show* in revenue generation. It must have felt sweet, after being let down by the Beeb: there's no revenge quite as gratifying as being proved right.

His service to British broadcasting was given royal approval in 1970 when Andrews was awarded a CBE (Commander of the Order of the British Empire). If anyone had dared to tease the ex-boxer for 'taking the Queen's shilling' when he first came over to the UK, they now had further ammunition after he took the Queen's bling, but, in fact, he was popular in Ireland as well, where it was recognized how much he had done for the new medium of television.

Eamonn Andrews represented the easy-going Irishman with an effortless charm that endeared him to the British public. He was perceived as warm and accessible, someone folks on the couch at home could relate to as they watched television with a pot of tea and a plate of biscuits. According to Terry Wogan, 'He brought to the business the qualities of intelligence, decency and honour, to which the public responded.' I also like the way he never tried to be the 'star'. He recognized that the show was about his guests and not about him, and he never tried to show them in anything but a favourable light. He was a man you could trust.

His achievement is all the more remarkable when you consider that he first appeared on British radio and TV during the 1950s and 60s, when there was huge anti-Irish prejudice in the UK. It was partly because of the old complaints that the Irish drank too much and were in thrall to the Pope, but the Troubles were also rumbling beneath the surface and about to erupt. In 1965, the leaders of North and South met for talks, prompting vociferous complaint, mistrust and accusations of 'cosying up to the enemy'. Events spun out of control as the 60s drew to a close and the predominant images of the Irish in the UK became those of men in balaclavas in the streets of Belfast, and worsening violence between the two communities. It was against this background that Eamonn Andrews appeared on British television and I think he did much to advance the case for Irish people in Britain. Terry Wogan is usually given the credit for being the respectable Irishman who showed the British people that terrorists were just a small, unrepresentative group of the population, but Andrews came first and paved the way. He was on the air throughout the worst atrocities of the 1970s, with his warm smile and easy charm.

Unlike some of the characters in this book, Eamonn wasn't adopted as an 'honorary Brit'; he was always perceived as Irish, as shown by the Alan Partridge-style 'compliment' in his obituary in *The Times* in London: 'Eamonn, clutching the big red book with the gold embossed inscription THIS IS YOUR LIFE, would pounce and utter to so-and-so, brogue in cheek, those immortal words: "dis is yur loife".'

TERRY WOGAN: the cheeky national treasure

Born 3 August 1938

Heard the one about the Irishman who reminded the British of what they could be at their best? His name was Terry Wogan.

– Allison Pearson

Ever since I was a child, Terry Wogan has figured on radio and television in some shape or form. When I was fifteen, we went on a school tour to London and were allowed to be part of the audience on the *Wogan* chat show. Sitting there as a young lad, I was struck by how casual Terry was, how easy he made it look – and what an enjoyable job he had. The more I saw of his work, the more my personal admiration for the man grew and I'm sure it's a lot to do with his influence that I now earn my living by chatting to people.

Alongside Eamonn Andrews, Terry was for decades considered an unofficial Irish ambassador in Britain. Even when Anglo-Irish relations were at their lowest ebb, Terry transcended any potential prejudices by staying calm and carrying on as one of Britain's best-loved broadcasters. So how did the lad from Limerick become a British national treasure? There must be something in the Limerick waters that has produced such an eclectic coterie of famous sons. Rugby stars, film stars and stars of the small screen have emerged from a city that has had a rough deal down through the decades. Read Frank McCourt's best-selling book *Angela's Ashes* if you want to understand the grim poverty of the town – but then remember that Richard Harris and our very own Terry Wogan hail from it.

Terry's father was a grocery shop manager and the family were comfortably off. His parents gave him a pragmatic worldview that would mould young Terry into the man he later became. Looking back on that parental influence, he reflected that he owed his success to 'good timing and being able to think on my feet – my single most [important] virtue – something I learnt from my mother'. He had the stern religious education of many of his compatriots but Wogan's parents had a no-nonsense approach to it that he carries to this day: 'Blind faith, and an unquestioning belief in the rantings of an apparently deranged priest, were just not a factor of everyday life in Limerick . . . People believed it . . . My father certainly didn't, and my mother's sense of humour wouldn't allow her to either.'

Terry was a good student with what he calls a 'butterfly brain' that produced a smart schoolboy, 'a little above average, I think they'd say, and mercifully, there's none of them alive to say more'. Away from the books, young Terry developed an interest in radio – but not the type that dominated most Irish homes at the time. He explained to me: 'What I think made me slightly different from my school mates was that they'd be listening to Radio Eireann and I'd be listening to the BBC Light Programme so my youth was formed by *Take It from Here, Much Blinding in the Marsh, The Goon Show*. All those BBC, if you like, West Brit things.' I should explain that 'West Brit' is an insult used about people considered too anglophile. You might be called it if you were seen to be affecting airs and graces, such as inviting someone for tea and scones (pronounced to rhyme with 'yawns' rather than 'stones'). No one could ever accuse Terry of this . . .

When he was fifteen, the Wogans moved to Dublin and Terry was sent to Belvedere, a prestigious institution that includes eleven alumni who were made knights of the realm. We'll wait a few paragraphs before we name the twelfth!

In his early twenties, he joined RTÉ as an announcer and newsreader. To get there, he had to pass an audition that required the applicant to be multi-lingual: 'Every brief-less barrister in the country was applying . . . there were very few decent jobs and I'm called for an audition and because I'm a good mimic, I can fake it. So I faked the Gaelic and I faked the Italian and I faked the German and somehow, I passed the audition!' He quickly earned the reputation of a 'messer' who distracted himself (and those around him) by setting fire to fellow presenters' scripts as they were being read out live on radio. On the day President John F. Kennedy drove through the streets of Dublin in June 1963, the commentator for the stretch that took in O'Connell Street was young Terry. As ecstatic crowds showered ticker tape on the president, he commented that 'the falling shreds of paper looked more like CIE bus tickets than ticker tape'.

It's likely that if he had stayed in Ireland and with RTÉ, Terry would have reached the very top of the tree but when his variety show, *Jackpot*, was dropped, the man with what can only be described as a laid-back ambition turned his eyes to the promise of what lay beyond the Irish Sea.

'It had struck me, even at the beginning of my career, that broadcasting was far too rigid in Ireland, but I suppose perhaps, given the smaller size of the country, the more rigid the broadcasting must be,' he said in a newspaper interview. This is a point he expanded on when we met for a chat one bright summer morning in 2012. I had just landed at Heathrow for a week to fill in for Chris Evans and went straight to BBC Western House to see Terry after his radio show. He met me at the door and we hopped into the back of his chauffeur-driven Bentley and I thought, 'He's done all right for himself!' We went to a tapas restaurant and over a long lunch and a good bottle of wine, Terry kindly told me about the Irish element of his broadcasting life.

A man clearly comfortable in his skin, he had plenty to say both on and off the record and so, on the record, the conversation went a bit like this: 'I came to a realization I mightn't have been the right kind of person to communicate on a daily level with the Irish populace. I kind of felt that I couldn't call people "me auld dote".' He explained that the stuffy nature of broadcasting at the time wouldn't allow that sort of thing. 'Also, don't forget, I'd grown up with BBC radio and for me the BBC was the great broadcasting organization and I thought I'd like to give it a try. I found RTÉ, wonderful as it was, slightly restrictive. Everything had to be bloody scripted, everything had to be written out and I remember reading about Dean Martin and a television show in the States where he didn't rehearse. He walked out and he made it up as he went along.'

It is the last part of that quote that would define the Wogan School of Broadcasting – don't over-think it. RTÉ was great but too structured. Eventually, audience size mattered enough for Terry's need to expand his broadcasting horizons: 'I couldn't see, as a broadcaster, why I should remain entertaining a small audience. I sent some tapes over to the BBC, which worked.'

The BBC leap was a big and blind one that could have gone pear-shaped but Terry was ready for change:

> I've never believed in standing still; my whole pro-fessional career has been one of change, and, if you like, risk-taking. I left Ireland in 1969, having established myself there on radio and television, for a thirteen-week contract with BBC Radio . . . It never occurred to me that the BBC might not renew my contract, and I might have to crawl back to Ireland under the cover of darkness. I'm not at all sure I'd take that same risk now.

Once he made the decision to leave Dublin, Terry made London his home and he meant it. He was happy to keep his links with Ireland but wasn't interested in being a homesick ex-pat who drank too much and sang dreary dirges late into the night: 'The only thing that used to drive me mad – the next generation doesn't do it, but the previous did – was when they'd say: "Are you going home for the summer?" This *is* home. Once I left Ireland and had the family here, I never thought of Ireland as home. I am very proud to be Irish and I don't see any reason to change, but this is home.'

Armed with a dry humour and a droll wit, Terry took to the BBC airwaves with aplomb. Like a few notables before him, Terry was recognizable thanks to his Irish accent, an asset that most entertainers who cross the Irish Sea find useful:

> I think it was George Bernard Shaw who said that as soon as one Englishman opens his mouth, another Englishman despises him. The Irish accent is classless to an English ear. Half the population thought I was Val Doonican, those who didn't thought I was Eamonn Andrews . . . but the point is, it's a classless accent so they don't know whether you've been educated at Eton or whether you've gone to a comprehensive . . . it worked to Eamonn Andrews' advantage and to mine.

In 1972 Terry became a permanent fixture as host of the breakfast show on BBC Radio 2, where his cheeky take on life became as important to his listeners as tea and toast. His army of TOGs (Terry's Old Guys and Girls) became a praetorian guard of fans who fed the programme and adored the presenter. For the record, they still do. His bright reign on Radio 2 in the 1970s coincided with a dark period for Anglo-Irish relations. As bombs killed innocent men and women enjoying a pint in Guildford and Birmingham, and as innocent Irishmen were being plucked from the streets and tortured in prison, Terry kept going, lilt intact, without ever apologizing for his Irishness.

In a pre-peace-process *Irish Independent* article, a commentator wrote: 'While the masked man with the ArmaLite and the bomb seemed to represent one concept of Ireland, the benign and pleasing mug of Terry Wogan always redeemed that picture.' Terry was an ambassador, albeit an unwitting one, whose presence on such a big stage acted as a national alter-ego for a troubled country; 'Terry became, in the public image in Britain, Mr. Ireland; the Irishman you could always rely on to be cordial, decent and well-mannered. Even people who swore they would never buy another ounce of Irish butter after a particularly repellent bombing still warmed to Wogan, and conceded that you couldn't blame the personal for the political.'

Speaking about those days many years later, Terry remembers being acutely aware of his Irishness at the time, especially as he had to broadcast just hours after the Birmingham bombing: 'I never tried to deny that I was Irish. I never tried to pretend that I was anything other than what I was. I tried to point out that it was not being done in my name, or in the name of any Irish person that I knew – but they were tough times.' He was pleased to get calls from Irish listeners in the UK thanking him for representing them and making things easier for them. Even when reminiscing about such dark times, Terry leavens the mix with a sunnier reflection when discussing the time he received a bomb threat in the post to Broadcasting House in central London. 'All the traffic stopped on Upper Regent Street and Oxford Circus. The only thing is, he couldn't have been a tremendously loyal listener because I was away on holiday!'

Television soon beckoned and Terry's need for a new challenge was sated courtesy of shows like *Come Dancing* and the enormously popular quiz show, *Blankety Blank*. There were only so many chequebooks and pens Terry could give out, and when the bosses came offering him a chat show, the stage was set for another step up the ladder. It was 1985 when he began presenting *Wogan* thrice-weekly and the Irishman became the most recognizable face in these islands for the best part of a decade. Three years into his tenure at the helm, Terry told the *Irish Times* about the difficulties involved in presenting such a show: 'It has to look easy, like a conversation. You can't be interested in all the guests. I'm not. It's fine with someone like, say, Tom Wolfe – but actors and actresses are often very hard work. Some of them are nothing without a script.' In this regard, Terry cites the actress Bette Davis as an example of the frustrating interview in the 'modern' era, where the 'plug' trumps content. 'She [Davis] could never understand why we had this convention where you didn't plug it immediately.' Miming the Davis drawl, he adds: 'When are you going to mention my book?' But the show became a fixture right after the evening news and got huge viewing figures.

At the same time, Terry began doing the TV commentary for the *Eurovision Song Contest* and his wry, sardonic take on the naff performers and judges made it a must-watch event. He broke through the guilt many felt watching such an event by being 'the dad on the couch', chipping in the kind of comments being made in TV rooms around the country. It was never mean but always a little bit bold. Again, very Terry.

When I asked how he had adjusted to life in Britain, Terry told me, somewhat controversially, that 'the Irish and English for all their differences are very alike and the Irish middle classes – to which I belong – have always aspired to being British.' This sort of comment might rankle with the white-collar readers of the *Irish Times* but in the back of their minds, they know there is some truth in it. Back in 1981 when Charles and Di got married, no one in

Ireland would admit to actually watching the wedding, but there were plenty who drew the curtains and sneaked a peak, then read about it later in a woman's magazine. You can see how times have changed by the fact that in 2011, post-peace process, lots of Irish women were unashamed to admit they were glued to William and Kate's wedding, analysing every last clutch bag and fascinator.

Most of the Irish back home were proud of Terry as he became the king of UK television but there were occasional naysayers. In 1986 one critic at the *Irish Independent* decided that Ireland's most famous export was destined for the dustbin: 'Terry Wogan is not a major talent, never was a major talent and never will be a major talent'. I don't agree – and the British public didn't either – but Terry's chat show was dropped by BBC bosses in 1992, simply because they felt it had run its course. Many in this position might have taken the news badly and abandoned ship but fortunately for Terry, confidence was never a problem: 'When we were growing up in Ireland the biggest sin, apart from sex, was vanity. It has always been a source of amazement that anybody came out of my generation in Ireland with any self-esteem whatsoever, but we did.'

He returned to the loving arms of Radio 2, where he gently cultivated an adoring audience that would grow and grow. With the passage of time and increasing affection from the public, Terry arrived at what might be called his Age of Recognition.

First up in 2005 was the call from Buckingham Palace offering Terry a knighthood. Listeners were delighted, with one offering to tape back Terry's ears 'lest the cold steel leave a lobe on the Palace carpet, while another suggested a small but serviceable device not unlike a stair-lift that would help me off my knees'. Following countless pieces of advice from all quarters, the day finally came and Terry explained the routine as only he can:

Bow the head, not the body, kneel on the cushion, head
up. Down comes the sword. Up you get, while they hand
Her Maj the doings on a cushion. She hands them over.
You speak when you're spoken to – not before. She's
'Your Majesty' and then 'Ma'am', as in 'jam', not 'warm'.
When she extends the royal hand, that's it. Back a couple
of paces, bow the head, exit stage left, perspiring gently
with no feeling below your knees.

And there you have it – a typically Wogan analysis of a high-end
to-do. It's the nearest most of us will get to a knighthood without
going through the gates, such is his pithy power of description.

When he eventually had his 'turn', Terry exchanged a few words
with Queen Elizabeth: 'She tells me she had listened to me on the
radio that morning, and I asked if she had heard me read out a
listener's offer of a sausage roll and a glass of Pinot if she'd agree
to turn on the Christmas lights at Great Yarmouth on her way to
Sandringham. She smiled, extended the hand, and I knew it was
time to back off. Bow and make myself scarce.' And with that,
Limerick's favourite son and Lord of the TOGs became a Knight
Commander and a Knight of the British Empire (he was allowed
to do this because of his dual Irish/British citizenship). You might
have thought the folks back home in Ireland would have a poke
about it. They remain a little uncomfortable with ennobled compatriots and feel it's all a little over the top and a little too British.
Bob Geldof (whom we'll discuss in Chapter 8) got a bit of ironic 'Sir
Bob' ribbing when he got his honorary title. Exceptions are made,
though, and Terry is one such.

Around the same time came the home crowd when Terry was
named Limerickman of the Year and in 2004 awarded an honorary

doctorate from the University of Limerick – however, the big one was still to come. It was announced that Terry was to be given the Freedom of Limerick – but, being Ireland, it didn't come without detractors kicking up a fuss. In the days before he was to receive the honour, a former local councillor objected to Terry's award on the basis of comments he had made in the *Glasgow Herald* in May 1980, when he referred to Limerick as 'a town of spires and gossip and lots of frustrated people' before adding that he couldn't 'think of any impressive women to come out of Limerick. But I suppose Limerick must have produced some influential nuns.'

But that was twenty-seven years previously and in 2007 Terry said, 'Limerick never left me; whatever it is, my identity is Limerick. I am so pleased that I am from Limerick.' With his credentials and credibility intact, he joined John F. Kennedy, Bill Clinton and Pope John Paul II on the list of those honoured with the Freedom of Limerick.

Arguably Ireland's greatest living export to the UK, Terry Wogan continues to self-deprecate his way through life. We'll give the last word to him as he talks about his fan mail:

> One of the more hurtful, yet perceptive letters I received lately was one that pointed out the oddity that those whom the British public revere and love are known universally by their first names: Cilla, Elton, Ant and Dec, John, George, Paul and Ringo. Those in the public eye that they hold in little regard, not to mention disgust, they know by their surnames: Hitler, Crippen, Chirac, every prime minister and football manager since Churchill and Ramsey, Mussolini, de Gaulle and, dammit, Wogan.

GRAHAM NORTON: the 'shiny Irish poof'
Born 4 April 1963

> When I left Ireland I could enjoy my Irishness more. I
> never felt Irish enough when I was in Ireland . . . I think
> it was about being a Protestant . . . just the people I saw
> on television, I didn't feel like one of them.

I haven't applied any hard and fast rules to the comparative lengths
of the biographies in this book. You might argue that the person
I've deemed worthy of six pages is not remotely as important as
the person about whom two pages are written – and fair game
to you. Even I was surprised by how much attention I ended up
giving to Graham Norton, but in many ways he epitomizes the
very modern relationship between Ireland and Britain. He had a
complicated childhood (Protestant, rural, latterly gay) that became
a hectic if difficult adulthood that ultimately became one of the
greatest success stories in the modern history of British entertainment. One of the reasons Graham gets such a lengthy write-up
is that he knows how to get attention. His whole career has been
about being noticed, being different – and being very good at what
he does.

In all the years Graham Norton has been interviewed and in-
terrogated about the countless shows he has presented, the same
subjects come up for discussion time and time again. Was it crap
being gay in Ireland? Was Ireland crap to grow up in? Is being
camp a lifestyle choice? Could the BBC 'handle' humour like that?
Are you paid too much? Are you in love? With whom? How many
nights a week do you . . . OK, you get the point. There is such an

emphasis on Graham's extracurricular activities that sometimes his abilities get swallowed up by what has happened to him on the way to the top. And yet, when you read the opening paragraph of his autobiography, it becomes clear why people like me are curious about the background of people like him: 'Childhood: dull. Oh yes, to the outsider looking in there was the cross-dressing, the bed-wetting, the moving house thirteen times, but for the little boy wearing his sister's dress, lying in a pool of his own piss, there was little sense of thrill.'

The problem with starting your story like that is that people want to know more and then they try to analyse you to death via poorly informed psychobabble. And so, Graham is insecure and vulnerable (that'll be the urine), he was always a camp queen (Hallowe'en) and he'll never settle (Dad was a salesman). And now, as I climb onto this ladder that'll take me down off the high moral ground, it is time to meet the man who has described himself as a 'shiny Irish poof'.

Graham William Walker was all over the place as a boy, thanks largely to the fact that his dad was a sales rep for Guinness (Mum was a housewife). Born in the Dublin suburb of Clondalkin, Graham ended up on an all-Ireland tour that saw him living variously in Tramore (County Waterford), Kilkenny and, ultimately, Bandon, County Cork, the town that would end up being 'home' whenever Ireland was mentioned. A Protestant in one of the world's most obsessively Catholic countries, Graham was always going to stand out whether he liked it or not. Life at a Protestant boarding school appears to have been rather uneventful, as he explained to me in a recent interview: 'I was . . . bored stiff . . . I remember just waiting to leave. I knew you didn't have to stay somewhere whereas I think, you know, another kid in another town might have thought this is just my lot, you know, fate has plonked me here but I knew that wasn't the case.'

To alleviate the ennui, Graham looked for distractions: 'Maybe I would have enjoyed it more if I'd had a social life. But I didn't. I just watched TV all the time.' Among the peculiar television offerings from RTÉ at the time that caught Graham's eye were *That Girl*, *The Philip Wilson Show* and the *Dick Cavett Show*, a chat show for the thinking man. Given how things turned out, maybe this wasn't such a bad thing but we'll get to that later.

Graham was keen to get out of school and into the real world: 'It never really crossed my mind that I would stay [in Bandon]. From an extraordinarily young age I sat around waiting to go: I mean really young, 10 or 11, I knew.' The fact that he was a Protestant would've been tough enough but being gay made it all so much tougher. In 1983, when Graham was twenty, it was still illegal to get divorced, to use a condom and to be gay. 'Ireland was an impossible place to be gay,' he said. 'Why would you be gay there? It would be like, "Now I'm gay, drinking my water in my gay way." Being gay is about sex, and there was nobody to have sex with. I would have been left dancing around my own handbag.' He had £200 and a desire for adventure so he went to San Francisco. Where else?

From Ireland's Kansas to America's Oz, Graham could enjoy himself and relax a little as most twenty-year-olds should but he was, he explained, an 'Irish twenty, which anywhere else in the world is about fourteen!' There was a story doing the rounds that Graham was a rent boy while there but the reality is that he applied for a job of one description, was asked to perform one of quite a different hue and promptly left the room. Of course, it would've been a salacious and delicious story if it had been true but, alas, it's now a colourful footnote that follows Graham to this day. At any rate, he didn't stick around to further his career in America and, given the ignorance about and prevalence of AIDS at the time, he looks back at his departure from San Francisco wistfully: 'San Francisco was a gay Disneyland. At the time, I was thinking: I should be having lots of sex, what's wrong with me? But looking back, it's like: Thank God!'

Graham headed to London where he successfully applied for a place at the Central School of Speech and Drama, and he graduated in 1989 together with a new name. There happened to be another actor called Graham Walker so he chose his great-grandmother's maiden name for his new identity, and with an ever-growing personality, Graham Norton set out to be a star.

The Troubles were still fomenting ancient and newly formed enmity between our countries, but Graham feels that the arts remained beyond the reach of sectarian hatred:

> The whole idea of Ireland being downtrodden by the Brits [is one thing] but at any given time, particularly in the arts, they were always wildly accepting. The playwrights, the artists, the novelists . . . there's always been a disproportionate number of very successful Irish people. It's odd. Whether that's something to do with the Irish or whether it's something to do with Britain's attitude to the Irish, I don't know.

Like so many wannabe actors, Graham ended up as a waiter, but unlike many waiters, it was the making of him. Camp and rude to customers, the punters couldn't get enough of him and when he placed a tea towel on his head to impersonate Mother Teresa of Calcutta, everything changed. Taking the mick out of one of

Ireland's most venerated religious figures led to the pub's owner encouraging his flamboyant waiter to put on a show in the room above the pub and it was there that Graham performed 'Mother Teresa of Calcutta's Grand Farewell Tour'. In the show, he portrayed the religious figure as a mad Irish housewife. The show went down well and he took it to the Edinburgh Festival Fringe, where things really took off. More shows followed and with pop icons like Karen Carpenter and Charlie's Angels featuring in his material, Graham was bringing camp to the masses. Andrew Martin, writing for the *Evening Standard*, likened him 'with his eye-rolling expressions of incredulity and rambling digressions' to 'an out of the closet Frankie Howerd'.

A brief but memorable turn in *Father Ted* brought Graham to the attention of Irish audiences in 1996 but he was still a relatively unknown rising star. This, however, was rapidly changing and while he was happy performing to ever-fuller houses in Britain, he would go on to develop a fear of playing to a 'home' crowd: 'I really am terrified of doing gigs in Ireland, and I don't know why . . . I just feel so exposed when I'm doing a show; I feel as if the people know me – or rather, know too much about me . . .' Perhaps it's because of that double handicap he had at home: being not just gay but Protestant to boot.

For whatever reason, Graham's schtick seemed to fit in Britain, a country that has always had a fondness for camp and for the occasional Irish accent. With him, they were getting two for the price of one. Like Eamonn Andrews and Terry Wogan, he has often remarked on the unthreatening nature of the Irish brogue: 'You know what they always say about having an Irish accent in Britain? It's as good as being classless because you don't fit in with their systems so you can be who you want to be and nobody knows any different.'

He told me: 'Whereas any British performer opens their mouth and the audience immediately is realigning themselves with the performer. They're going "Am I posher than them, am I less posh than them, did I go to a better school?" They're doing all of that just by the sound of their voice and with an Irish person, it's kind of a clean slate so you can talk to a mainstream audience.'

In 1997, he was nominated for the Perrier Award at the Fringe but was beaten to it by the League of Gentlemen. It didn't really matter as Graham was now being noticed, and after he won a British Comedy Award following a five-week stint as a stand-in chat show presenter, Channel 4 were first out of the traps with a job offer and *So Graham Norton*, an unconventional and innovative take on the chat show, was born. It was camp, it was outrageous, almost hedonistic in a lascivious, leering way. With its knowing wink and borderline filth, it was refreshingly different. One critic described Graham as 'a 21st-century Larry Grayson with access to the web'. It could be seen on Irish TV but never raised the ire of the Church authorities as Dave Allen had done. Although he wasn't averse to a bit of Church-knocking, it was almost three decades on from when Allen was thrown off RTÉ and times had changed a bit.

Within three years, the show was beating *The Weakest Link* and *Who Wants to be a Millionaire?* at the BAFTAs. Multi-million pound deals were signed and Graham Norton was among the most recognizable names in Britain. Enormously successful chat shows followed on Channel 4, then there was a lucrative move to the BBC where a career hiatus of sorts ensued, with neither Graham nor the organization for whom he worked quite certain as to what the next step might be.

It was round this time that the 'Are you paid too much?' questions showered down and he developed a 'line' on which he riffed when the query arrived: 'That salary is a miracle. I don't know how I get it. But if the BBC has decided that's my market value, then what kind of moron would go: "No! Please take half of my salary and invest in Saturday morning children's programmes!"'

A dance show and a couple of reality/talent shows were all fine and very dandy but when Jonathan Ross's ship ran aground, Graham found another home on Friday night television, where healthy ratings see him on top of the talent heap. He has also taken over Terry Wogan's crown as the cynical *Eurovision* presenter and has worn it well.

Graham's relationship with Ireland improved too, and his purchase of a home on West Cork's Sheep's Head peninsula allows him a bolt-hole from the intensity of London.

A semi-tortured relationship with his hometown has mellowed into one of great warmth and very real connection. This may have begun when Graham's dad died and the good people of Bandon showed their true colours to their prodigal son. He wrote:

> Almost as soon as we got back from the nursing home the doorbell started to ring. Neighbours who had heard the news came to pay their respects. They brought cakes, they brought bottles of whiskey, but mostly they brought their memories of my father. Far from being intrusive or insensitive, as I thought such visits would be, they were wonderfully comforting . . . That sense of community and support brought me a whole new respect and affection for Ireland. All the things that I had thought were there to hold me back I now found were there to hold me up.

Bandon had plans to honour him by erecting a statue but Graham begged them not to – 'such a waste of money and it would look hideous' – so they are naming a riverside walkway after him instead. He's also recently been awarded an honorary doctorate by University College Cork, which left him 'surprised' but thrilled.

He mused to me that age might have something to do with his changing attitude to Ireland: 'As I get older, I don't know why, certainly I spend a lot of time here now which, to the boy who ran off to Paris and London, if you told him he would, you know, willingly, come back here and spend months at a time, he wouldn't have believed you . . . I enjoy it more. Mind you, I have money now!'

Arguably Britain's most prized broadcasting asset of the twenty-first century so far, the boy from Bandon has reached the top of the ladder and as he begins his fifties with a spring in his step, we can only wonder – where next for Mr Norton? Of course, he has plans of his own: 'I always say I will end my days sitting in bed with my BAFTAs, dribbling soup down myself, which my dogs lick off, watching daytime telly.'

DES LYNAM: a smooth operator
Born 17 September 1942

A common misperception of me is . . . I'm from the English middle classes when I'm from Irish working classes.

In many respects, Des Lynam is one of the most 'English' of the Irish-born subjects in this book. Of all the names I mention to people, his is the one that gets the most 'Oh, really? I didn't know he was Irish!' (Michael Gambon – see Chapter 7 – is a close second.) In fact, Lynam only just makes it into the book. His parents had left for Britain before he was born but when the Second World War began, his father, a nurse, was called up for service and posted to Northern Ireland. When Des was conceived, his mother Gertrude, also a nurse, decided to head home to Ennis in County Clare to be near her family for the birth and so Britain's best-loved sportscaster is an Irishman from the west of Ireland.

A sister, Ann, came soon afterwards but died in infancy from meningitis. Grief-stricken, the Lynams packed their bags and took their son back to Brighton after the war where they eventually secured a council house. Of his early childhood, Des says, 'I had a very good life . . . I was looked after, fed well and all the rest of it, we weren't poverty-stricken but . . . we had no money.'

Initially it was a tough transition for young Des, whose thick Irish accent was ridiculed by his peers. 'I didn't go to school in Ireland at all but at school [in England] I had a very broad, not only Irish but Clare accent, so much so that the neighbours here couldn't understand a single word I said and neither could they at school but of course at that sort of age, at five years of age, you adjust very quickly and you start talking like your peers very, very rapidly and I think the Irish accent disappeared within about six months.'

When we chatted for this book, Des told me of an event that had such an effect on him at an early age that the detail still remains vivid: 'The teacher said, "Right, everybody, draw a line." Well for me, a line was the same as a tiger or an elephant and so I drew a funny little animal with a mane and she came around and gave me a little tap on the hand with the ruler . . . I thought, "What the hell is going on here?"'

A septic appendix didn't help enamour him to his new home country either: 'I didn't like this place called England. First they mocked the way you speak, and then you got hit with not one, but two serious illnesses at once. I wanted to go back to Ireland.'

His wish was granted – but only once a year, when the family took the ferry back to Ireland, where Des spent his summers ducking between showers while his classmates worked on their sunburn on Brighton beach. But Des loved his holidays in Ireland and hated going home: 'I used to cry when we came back . . . Life there was so special for me because I was in the bosom of my mother's family – grandparents, uncles and aunts and nephews and nieces. We used to congregate together so it was always great company whereas back in England I was an only child.'

Des went into the insurance business on leaving school in the early 1960s. It was as good a place as any for someone who had a knack for idle banter but not for a would-be performer who had his sights set on a wider audience. That all started with a stint as a sports reporter for BBC Radio Brighton, and within six months he was called to the mother ship at BBC HQ in London, where he was offered a job as a sports assistant before becoming presenter on *Sports Report* in 1969 at the age of twenty-six. He was filling shoes that had, five years earlier, been vacated by Eamonn Andrews.

Lynam went on to become a boxing commentator, and one of his jobs was following Muhammad Ali around the world. By 1977, he was transferred to television, where his smooth delivery and even smoother style secured him a place in the corner of the British public's sitting rooms for decades to come.

First up was *Sportswide*, a show he anchored for six years, followed by *Grandstand*, the iconic show Lynam made his own. Along the way he picked up the affectionate nickname of 'Silver Fox' and became the subject of friendly ridicule by mimics everywhere who donned fake moustache and laid-back voice to take off the much-loved broadcaster. 'He is neither urban nor rural, but rather something in between – say, Surrey or the Cotswolds. He is the man you meet in a pub on a Sunday lunchtime. His Jaguar XK8 – that is, indeed, his car – will be parked outside,' read a *Sunday Times* profile.

It was around this time that comedian Mrs Merton memorably described Des as 'the menopausal woman's Tom Cruise'. It was a hilarious description that did him no harm at all, but even when there was criticism Des was well able to roll with the punches, explaining: 'Being Irish puts things into perspective. I don't think you take life too seriously.'

Des took over another iconic show in 1988 when he started presenting *Match of the Day*, and soon he was also covering Wimbledon and myriad World Cups, Olympics and Grand Nationals. In 2005, he migrated to the cult quiz show *Countdown* following the death of its much-loved presenter Richard Whiteley and presented that for eighteen months. Now he continues to work on specials and documentaries at what appears to be his own pace in his own time.

During his years on British screens Des has gone in and out of fashion. He's quite jazzy and old school so for a while he was considered a little cheesy, then there was the irony period heralded by Mrs Merton and the mimics, then post-irony, and now he's just generally respected and liked. Personally, I admire his ability to make television look easy. He knows how to look in the camera, and he also has the charm of the Irish, particularly knowing how to make women feel special. He's very proud of his Irishness, and often holidays back in the country of his birth, although he has never had a show on Irish television.

I don't think I'd go as far as Johnny Vaughan, who said in 1999: 'There have been three great white entertainers, Presley, Sinatra and Lynam. With Frank's death, Des is left to carry the torch.' He was a proficient sports presenter with an easy, laid-back style but I certainly have never heard him sing. What interests me is that many would consider him quintessentially English. As the *Sunday Times* profile said, 'It may seem odd . . . that he is Irish by birth. But Vladimir Nabokov and Joseph Conrad wrote great, original English because it was not their first language. So Des becomes English because he instinctively retains the very awareness the English have lost – the sense of Englishness as a distinct, definable phenomenon.'

ZIG and ZAG: furry *agents provocateurs*
Born 1987

'Never mind the zogabongs . . .'

The only brothers to make it into this book also happen to be aliens. And they also happen to be puppets. Born on the planet Zog, the cheeky duo Zig and Zag started life in 1987 on RTÉ television as furry sidekicks to the genial human presenter, Ian Dempsey. For five years, they defined afternoon television for children, semi-sober students and those unemployed people with a sense of humour. I was in my teens when they first appeared on our screens and watched, bemused, as their show became cult TV. At the peak of their fame in Ireland, the cuddly toy versions of Zig and Zag were in such demand that Santa nearly handed in his resignation.

In 1992, the Zagabonds landed their UFO in Britain as regulars on Channel 4's *The Big Breakfast*. As brazen sidekicks to Chris Evans (at his most marvellously manic) these were halcyon mornings for British breakfast television. Like Miss Piggy and Kermit before them, they are able to say and do things that humans would consider beyond the pale. They have a particularly bold charm and blurt out all those things us other chat show hosts would love to be able to say but would probably get sacked for, such as 'You're a thundering bore and I'm going to try to find a way to wrap up this interview as soon as possible.'

Zig and Zag went on to appear on MTV and ITV before returning most recently to Ireland, where they fronted an outtakes show, *Zig and Zag Superbloopers*.

Known formally as Zigmund Ambrose Zogly and Zagnatius Hillary Zogly, their 'minders', Ciaran Morrison and Mick O'Hara, are rather shy Dubliners who prefer to let their charges do the talking. When they came on the *Late Late Show* I felt it was one of those nostalgic privileges. They are almost impossible to interview as they are so giddy and keen to catch you out. Eyeballing a puppet and trying to ask questions on live television is strangely not that easy; I'll take a beleaguered prime minister any day!

Zig and Zag's Irishness is just part of their cheekiness. They could have been Scottish or Welsh, but I suppose if you're going to be a smart-arsed alien made of fur you might as well come from Ireland. Perhaps coming from over the water gives slightly more of a licence to shock . . .

*　　*　　*

It's interesting that the British have adopted quite so many Irish chat show hosts over the decades but I think it's down to our image as genial, cheeky and charming. There's a twinkle in the eye as the difficult question is asked and even if there is a bit of argy-bargy on screen the viewer can imagine we're all friends having a beer in the green room afterwards (which is usually, but not always, the case . . .). Like most of my countrymen, I love meeting new people and having a chat, so being paid to chat for a living has always seemed to me a particularly fortuitous career.

What other job is there where you get paid for talking? Oh yes, politics. Well, we haven't exported many politicians to Britain over the centuries, for obvious reasons, but there are a few notable exceptions I'll describe in the next chapter.

4

POLITICIANS, SOLDIERS and REPORTERS

BEFORE THE SECOND HALF of the twentieth century the vast majority of Irish émigrés were the dispossessed, lacking money, opportunity and hope. Many looked west to America but huge numbers turned their gaze towards the streets of London, which, according to the nursery rhyme, were paved with gold. With such an influx you might have expected some pushy souls to finagle their way into the British political system, but hardly any tried. One of the main reasons was simply economic: you needed to be well off to enter politics because until 1911 MPs weren't paid salaries. Another was religious: it wasn't until the Catholic Relief Act of 1829 that Catholics could vote, and even then it was only the wealthy ones. Catholics weren't allowed in the judiciary or the civil service either. The odds were stacked against them, and with growing anti-British feeling back home not many wanted to take their chances. That's why it's all the more interesting that there were a few intrepid souls who ventured over to try their hand at British politics and made a significant impact.

There were 200,000 Irish soldiers battling it out in the trenches in the First World War, when Ireland was still part of the United Kingdom, but most Irish felt the Second World War was nothing to do with them. Eamon de Valera, who led Ireland's struggle for independence from British rule, was Taoiseach when Britain declared war on Nazi Germany. He argued that the Irish had only just managed to unshackle themselves from the British in 1921 and that they couldn't establish themselves as an independent geographic and political entity if they jumped every time a British prime minister snapped his fingers. A minority of the Irish felt they should have played a part in trying to defeat Nazism, but the government aimed to be neutral. Eamon de Valera even signed the book of condolence when Hitler died – a move that didn't do an awful lot for Anglo-Irish relations.

De Valera's views weren't universally shared in the Irish army, though, and almost 5,000 brave souls broke ranks and defied the government to cross the sea and wear the British army uniform during the Second World War. I'm sure many of them were idealists and wanted to fight against fascism and anti-Semitism, but I suspect at least some just wanted an adventure. At the time they were labelled deserters, but – as it has in so many other areas the peace process has brought about a sea change in attitudes. In May 2013 all those men were finally pardoned by the Irish Minister of Justice, who said this act should remove 'any tarnish from their name or reputation'. It was sixty-eight years after the war ended so the gesture was largely symbolic: while it comforted the families of the fallen, the soldiers themselves had all died as deserters in the eyes of the Irish state.

While the Irish may not have had much political influence in the UK, there have always been Irish journalists coming over to comment on British politics, right back to Jonathan Swift, the satirist who lashed out mercilessly at hypocrisy in all its forms and was equally happy writing pamphlets attacking the Whigs or the Tories.

In one of his best-known works, the *Modest Proposal*, he suggests that the Irish might ease their economic troubles by selling their children to the rich as food. He even goes on to suggest some cooking methods. It's one of the most powerful pieces of satire in the English language. There's more about Swift in Chapter 6, but I mention him here as one in a long line of Irish wordsmiths who've come over to sharpen their pens on UK affairs.

First of all, we're going back in time to the eighteenth century to meet a man who in his ideas and actions seems so modern he could be at home in the present day (give or take the frock coats and the funny hairstyle).

EDMUND BURKE: an eloquent humanist

12 January 1729–9 July 1797

The only thing necessary for the triumph of evil is for the good to do nothing.

Henry VIII had a lot to answer for. One of the side effects of his split from the Church of Rome so that he could get Anne Boleyn into the sack was that centuries later Catholics were still cast into the role of second-class citizens who were unable to practise in many of the professions. Edmund Burke's father was a Dublin solicitor and always claimed to be a practising Anglican because he couldn't have done the job as a Catholic. In turn, he told everyone he brought up his son as an Anglican – although his sister was brought up a Roman Catholic, like his mother. Complicated business. This would all become controversial later when Burke's political enemies tried to spread the rumour that he was secretly a Catholic and as such not permitted to stand for political office. He denied he was a Catholic, the hurdle was overcome and he became a member of the British Parliament in 1765, where he soon became renowned for the eloquence of his speeches. He spoke 'in such a manner as to stop the mouths of all Europe', commented the Prime Minister, William Pitt (the Elder), after his maiden speech; I suspect there's a compliment in there somewhere.

Among the many causes that Burke championed, he argued vociferously that Parliament should limit the power of the monarch and put a ceiling on their expenses – thereby diminishing his chances of a knighthood and the acquisition of a bit of land somewhere in the shires. He believed that effective government of the people required cooperation between rulers and their subjects, and was opposed to the taxes imposed on the Americans that finally caused them to have a tea party in Boston Harbor. (That's the tea party that sparked a revolution and inspired an expression that still resonates in America to this day.) He tried to stop corruption among those governing India, saying that colonial rule should be by the consent of those being ruled: 'All government, indeed every human benefit and enjoyment, every virtue, and every prudent act, is founded on compromise and barter.' During the French Revolution, he was one voice sounding a note of caution about the dangers of mob rule and telling them to cut down on the guillotining. And he strongly argued for the rights of Irish Catholics to worship and work alongside their Protestant compatriots, despite the unpopularity of the cause: 'Toleration is good for all, or it is good for none.'

The range of his beliefs meant that he wasn't aligned with either the Whig or the Tory party: he just said it (or wrote it) as he saw it, and it is for this that I am proud to hail him as a great Irish export. His arguments that the constitution should be structured so as to prevent any one person or party gaining a tyrannical hold on power, and that members of Parliament should not be aligned to specific interests but should be free to vote as their conscience dictates, are ones that have had huge influence down the years. And maybe some twenty-first-century figures should go back and have a cursory read of his writings. I think he was able to say all this because he was outside the mainstream of British politics – and people listened to him simply because he said it so well.

ARTHUR WELLESLEY, 1st Duke of Wellington: the Iron Duke

1 May 1769–14 September 1852

Being born in a stable does not make one a horse.

Arthur Wellesley is probably the most reluctant recruit to the Anglo-Irish story. The man born in Dublin coined the phrase about being born in a stable not making you a horse in response to the 'accusation' that he was Irish. According to him, the accident of his place of birth did not define him since everything else about him was profoundly British – but I beg to differ, and so does the passport office!

Poor Arthur was born on Merrion Street but came from a very landed Protestant family that owned Dangan Castle, set in an extraordinary 13,700 acres in lush County Meath. Of course, it wasn't long before he was bound for Eton College and then to the Academy of Equitation at Angers in France (a finishing school stroke military academy), from which he emerged as 'an Irish lad of great promise' according to his teachers.

By 1790, Arthur had become MP for his home village of Trim,

County Meath, and thereafter sought and attained military glory in India and Egypt. These successes earned him a knighthood in 1804. Keen to maintain a political interest alongside his martial endeavours, Arthur was appointed Chief Secretary for Ireland in 1807, an important posting given the rebellious unrest that had surfaced in 1798 and again in 1803. The reluctant Irishman was intent on bolstering defences to strengthen the union and was completely opposed to Irish nationalism.

At this point Arthur was married to Catherine Pakenham, daughter of the 2nd Baron Longford. They'd been close as teenagers but when he went back to marry her in 1806, he found her changed and said to his brother, somewhat ungallantly, 'She has grown ugly, by jove.' The marriage went ahead and they had two sons, but rumours of his fondness for other ladies appear to be well founded.

Further military success followed against the French in 1809, thus earning Arthur a pecrage and, with it, a name change. The lad from Trim was now Viscount Wellington. His record against the French led to more advancement and by 1814 he was made a duke and handed £400,000 by Parliament as a nineteenth-century golden handshake.

A brief stint as British ambassador to Paris was interrupted by Napoleon's dramatic escape from exile on the island of Elba. Arthur was put in joint command of the army sent to defend Brussels from a French invasion. It was he who confronted Napoleon at the village of Waterloo in June 1815. His troops held their ground until the Prussians arrived and together they drove Napoleon into retreat. Within a matter of weeks, Napoleon had abdicated and Wellington was a national icon. The phrase 'meeting one's Waterloo' has come to mean facing a great and decisive challenge after which one side is proclaimed victorious and the other utterly annihilated. You'll often hear sports presenters misuse it, but the battle it referred to was one of the great British military victories of all time.

In 1827, Arthur was made commander-in-chief of the British army and just a year later, he became British Prime Minister, a post he held from 1828–30 and again for three weeks in 1834. He served as foreign secretary under Robert Peel and retired from public life in 1846.

Correspondence from this time shows Arthur as a loyal British subject who was utterly convinced that Ireland should be 'kept down' and constantly talked of defending the country of his birth for the crown. He did speak out passionately in support of Catholic Emancipation, but he was against the 1832 Reform Act because it gave the vote to far too many poor people. He was said to have been nicknamed the 'Iron Duke' because of the iron shutters he had to install in his London house after angry mobs who wanted the vote came to smash his windows. (He also gave his name to wellington boots and a rather delicious dish of beef in pastry known as a Beef Wellington.)

In Dublin, an obelisk to his memory is a focal point for picnics and other less tasteful pursuits in Phoenix Park, but the Irish don't often claim credit for one of their countrymen winning the Battle of Waterloo – and I think it's about time we did. He'd hate that!

BRENDAN BRACKEN: the original Big Brother

15 February 1901–8 August 1958

Everything about you is phoney. Even your hair, which looks like a wig, isn't.

– An acquaintance of Bracken

Ireland's fractious relationship with its nearest neighbour has always been bedevilled by a push-pull dynamic that sees many Irish lured by the best of Britain but then forced to endure the cat calls from those who stayed behind and accuse the departed of 'taking the Queen's shilling' as if they had betrayed our country for another. My next subject is another man who, like Wellington, buried his roots to great effect and embedded himself in the heart of the British political establishment with no concern at all as to what his compatriots thought of him. Bold, brash Brendan Bracken abandoned the auld sod, 'took the shilling' and lived a remarkable life along the way. This is his extraordinary tale . . . .

Bracken is possibly this book's best-kept secret and, given the nature of the man, it isn't so surprising. Bracken liked to keep secrets – lots of them. But his tenuous relationship with the truth took him all the way from rural Ireland to 10 Downing Street by way of Australia. So, how did the boy from Templemore, County Tipperary, end up as Viscount Bracken, Winston Churchill's eyes and ears during the Second World War?

Brendan was born the third of four children into the family of a builder, Joseph Bracken. His father died when he was three and then, when he was seven, the family moved to Dublin, where Brendan stood out as a smart but naughty child, changing schools a couple of times before being sent to boarding school in Limerick. This failed to improve his behaviour as Brendan had a propensity to truant from school, preferring the comforts of a local hotel where he ran up costly bills. That was enough for his mother and the young Brendan was dispatched to a family friend in Australia.

Life Down Under was as charmed as Brendan could make it. He worked as a sheep farmer and as a teacher in various schools. A keen reader and blessed with a silver tongue, he rambled around

Australia, making friends randomly and finessing his schtick by way of self-reinvention.

By the time Brendan decided to head for England, he had a CV that was an extraordinary work of fiction. He claimed he was Australian, a graduate and then, in 1920, aged nineteen, he pretended to be a fifteen-year-old orphan whose parents had been killed in a bush fire back 'home' in Australia – which lie gained him admittance to Sedbergh public school.

By the end of 1922, Brendan was working as a journalist and began to make connections that would change his life. The most important of these was with Winston Churchill, who took Brendan on board as an election staffer in 1923–4.

He moved quickly through socially and politically important pools. A great man for the bon mot, he cut a peculiar figure, and the rumour that he was Churchill's illegitimate son began to do the rounds. When Churchill's wife questioned Winston on the story, he playfully responded: 'I looked it up but the dates don't coincide!'

Bracken didn't look at all like Churchill. In fact, he was extraordinary-looking with, as his biographer Charles Lysaght describes, 'A big pale face, a slightly flattened nose, wire spectacles, blackened teeth, and a shock of crinkly carrot-coloured hair which sat on his head like a bad wig. His accent was hybrid Irish-Australian-cockney.' For those who queried the background of this arriviste, he usually maintained the story of the Australian bush fire and certainly never let on that he had a mother and siblings back in Ireland.

Brendan's journalistic career thrived throughout the 1920s, by the end of which he was earning the very comfortable salary of £30,000 per annum as editor of *The Banker*, chairman of the *Financial News*, and managing director of *The Economist*.

In 1929, Brendan became MP for North Paddington. Just. But it was enough to get him into that chamber of politics and power and he made sure to get close and stick by his old mentor, Churchill, becoming his private secretary in 1939 when his boss was made First Lord of the Admiralty. Brendan's role for Churchill appears to have been a mixed bag of dogsbody, policy guru, advisor, tell-tale and friend. He has been described as the original spin-doctor, an early prototype Alastair Campbell, and had plenty of enemies as befits that role.

Bracken was duly rewarded for his tenacious loyalty by being appointed Minister of Information in 1941. It was Britain's darkest, most dangerous hour and the voice of this country at war was a red-haired Irishman who everyone thought was either Australian or Churchill's bastard son. He was neither but he proved adept at his job. For a brief moment Bracken was First Lord of the Admiralty and he was later made Viscount Bracken of Christchurch in 1952. He never took his seat in the House of Lords, a place he waspishly referred to as 'The Morgue'.

Other Bracken-related rumours include the suggestion that George Orwell was referring to him (courtesy of his initials) when he coined the phrase 'Big Brother' to describe the dystopian state government in his brilliantly bleak *1984*. Charles Lysaght suggests that Evelyn Waugh based the character of Rex Mottram in *Brideshead Revisited* on the Irish/Australian/Englishman: 'a fast-talking, social-climbing colonial bounder who knows everyone and can fix everything'.

Having made generous donations to Sedbergh, the school he spoofed his way into, Brendan continued to dabble in journalism and the education system. He hated socialism and memorably called Aneurin Bevan a 'Bollinger Bolshevik', a 'Ritzy Robespierre' and a 'lounge lizard Lenin'. Churchill's son Randolph described Bracken as 'the fantasist whose fantasies had come true'. In 1958, Bracken contracted throat cancer and as he lay dying in his Park Lane flat, he still managed to quip about a cleric his friend had brought along: 'The blackshirts of God are after me.'

An unorthodox figure, perhaps one of his most important contributions to British history was in keeping Winston Churchill buoyed up during the war, and helping to drag him out of his famous 'black dog' depressions. According to Harold Macmillan, they 'quarrelled and argued incessantly, just like a happily married couple', and Bracken's astute descriptions of participants in the war, such as calling General Montgomery 'a master of caution in all things except speech', kept the boss entertained. So we can claim that an Irishman played a significant role in Britain winning the Second World War, despite our official national no-show.

While Bracken fought the war on the ground, another Irishman was busy doing the same thing but in the air. It's time to meet Brendan 'Paddy' Finucane, RAF superstar.

BRENDAN 'PADDY' FINUCANE: flying ace

16 October 1920–15 July 1942

> If ever I feel a bitter feeling rising in me about the Irish, the hands of heroes like Finucane seem to stretch out to soothe them away.
>
> – Winston Churchill, 1948

Researching this book has thrown up a few surprises for me and none more than the one we're about to encounter. Anglo-Irish history was fraught in the extreme up until very recently. When I studied history at school, there was no mention of the Irishmen who got slaughtered at the Somme and all over Europe in the First World War and not a word about the Irishmen who contributed to the noble struggle to defeat the threat of Nazi Germany in the Second World War. It wasn't discussed in the classroom and it certainly wasn't written about in our textbooks. There was a Hibernian 'omertà' on the subject of the Irish boys who took the 'King's shilling' at a time when we were fighting for our freedom in the first instance and trying to establish our independence in the second.

I remember speaking to a Franciscan friar, Brother Columbanus Deegan, whom I met when doing a radio report on the making of the movie *Saving Private Ryan*. Colum was asked by Steven Spielberg to come to the beach in Wexford where they were filming the D-Day landings scene and verify the set-up was accurate, as he had been there the first time around. By the time I met Colum he was an older man but with a zest for life, dressed in dramatic brown robes that made him look like Obi-Wan Kenobi. We spoke of his life in Dublin back in 1940 and how he wanted adventure. This led him to the British army, where he was given a Harley Davidson and told to fix planes that had been shot down. He rode across Europe on his motorbike, watching comrades getting killed and cities being razed. He saw concentration camps being liberated and Nazism being defeated. When he returned to Dublin, Colum had to keep his head down and say nothing about where he had been. His 'like' were not appreciated and his chosen path was considered treacherous. When the peace process, culminating in the Good Friday Agreement, bedded down, there was a new attitude to Colum and those like him. As Bertie Ahern and Tony Blair mixed it up with Martin McGuinness and Ian Paisley, Irish history was revisited and Presidents Robinson and McAleese led the way for Irish people to remember old relatives who had British army medals hidden away in biscuit tins out of state-sponsored shame. Colum was brought to Normandy to celebrate the fiftieth anniversary of the D-Day landings in 1994. History had corrected itself.

One of my personal favourites in this selection of Hibernian heroes is the unlikely life of Brendan Finucane. I'd never heard of him before I started my research, but his story in many ways illustrates the absurdity of the seething enmity that for too long existed between two such close neighbours.

To begin, we need to revisit 1916 and Boland's Mill. This building was venerated for many years as the place Eamon de Valera occupied during the Easter Rising in 1916. Among the young men at his beck and call was one Thomas Andrew Finucane, father of Brendan. He was lucky to escape all the executions and internments the British ordered to punish participants; De Valera was sentenced to death but later had his sentence overturned and was released in 1917.

Four years after the rebellion and with hatred for the British still very much in the air, Brendan Finucane was born in the well-to-do Dublin suburb of Rathmines. Brendan was a good student and an active sportsman. A brief spell in hospital led to an unusual but prescient prediction. Brendan's mother, Florence, was told that a psychic was in the bed opposite and she cajoled him into predicting Brendan's fate. After some reluctance, the fortune-teller told her that the boy would meet a watery death by the age of twenty-one. Not a nice thing to hear about your firstborn!

When he was sixteen, Brendan and his family took the mail boat from Dun Laoghaire to Holyhead and travelled on to Surrey, where they began a new life. Two years later, Brendan joined the

RAF. It was 1938 and the winds of war were brewing in the skies of Europe. It wasn't long before he acquired the rather unimaginative nickname of 'Paddy' and it stuck. (It didn't have the pejorative overtones it would acquire later in the twentieth century, but was the equivalent of Tommy for an Englishman or Taffy for a Welshman.) The young man didn't seem to care about the nickname and paraded his Irishness with considerable pride, going so far as to have a shamrock placed alongside his initials on the Spitfire aeroplane that would bring him his moment in history.

Paddy took to the skies (and the war) with enthusiasm and ability. Despite his youth, he was considered leadership material from early on and as the war proceeded, Paddy and his Flying Shamrock became the stuff of legend. He spent most of his time in the skies above France, harassing German supply lines. Of his chosen career, Paddy said: 'I shoot to hit the machine, not the lad in it; at least, I hold him no grudge, but I have to let him have it. See him first before he sees you, hit him as you fire as you may not have a second chance.'

Such derring-do saw Paddy shoot down eleven German planes in one month alone. His progress up the ranks was meteoric so that by June 1942, at the age of twenty-one, he had been promoted to Wing Commander.

He explained modestly: 'I've been blessed with a pair of good eyes and I've learned to shoot straight' – but that didn't mean he was untouchable. In February 1942, he was conducting a daytime sweep over Dunkirk when a German gunner shot a shell through the Flying Shamrock's cockpit. Paddy remembered the event vividly: 'The cockpit was awash with blood. It was not until I was feeling a bit sick and dizzy did it dawn on me that it was my blood! Good Dublin blood should not be wasted . . . How I even managed to land without a crack-up will never be known, luck of the Irish triumphed that day if ever!'

Within weeks, the plane was fixed and Paddy was up in the air once more. Such was his fame that models of the Flying Shamrock were in demand along Piccadilly Circus and headlines announced with unbridled excitement 'Finucane Flies Again'.

It was just five months later when the Irishman's luck finally ran out. As he flew low over the beach at Pointe du Touquet, his radiator was hit and the plane crash-landed into the English Channel. Paddy's last words by radio were 'This is it chaps' before he landed, at the age of twenty-one, in his watery grave. The fortune-teller's prediction had been spot on.

It took the Irish media a few days to report the death of the unlikely war hero. Amid stories of U-boats and Panzers, and squeezed between reports of pig prices and Parliament rising for three months, the *Irish Independent* buried two paragraphs beneath the headline 'Air Ace Killed'. Working from an Air Ministry News Service press release, the paper told its readers that Wing Commander Finucane DSO DFC (with three bars) was 'drowned in the English Channel when his plane was shot from a German machine gun on the beach near Pointe de Touquet'. It didn't begin to do justice to his achievements.

In just two years, Brendan 'Paddy' Finucane had brought down thirty-two enemy planes in the aerial cauldron of war. It was a phenomenal record from the son of a 1916 veteran and fully justified Winston Churchill's praise, uttered in the midst of a 1948 tirade against Irish neutrality during the war.

From the mean streets of 1916 Dublin to the Luftwaffe-filled skies above wartime France, the Irish and British story continued to wrap itself around each other in an unending, unlikely bind.

ORLA GUERIN: the voice of truth

Born 15 May 1966

I'm the anti-stereotype, the Irish hack who doesn't drink.

If Irish journalists failed to give Paddy Finucane his due back in 1942, later in the century Ireland would give Britain a journalist who walks through fire to get at the truth. Hair pinned back and donning a flak jacket under a dusky sun somewhere in the world, Orla Guerin is an old-school reporter who practises proper pre-social-media journalism. She doesn't have a www dot in front of her name, doesn't do bells and whistles, but she gets herself out there in the streets of the world's highest-tension hotspots and tells it like it is in an earnest, no-nonsense style.

Orla is Dublin-born and qualified as a journalist from the Dublin College of Commerce in 1985. She started her career in newspapers before, at the age of twenty-three, becoming RTÉ's youngest-ever foreign correspondent. Her first posting was to Moscow, from where she covered the world-changing events in Eastern Europe in the early 1990s when the Balkan War was in full swing, and won a Jacob's Award in 1992 for her radio reports.

In 1994, she left RTÉ to run as a Labour party candidate in elections to the European parliament and did reasonably well, although she didn't win. Her stellar career continued in 1995 when Guerin was snapped up by the BBC and began the peripatetic lifestyle she has lived ever since: Los Angeles in 1996, then on to Rome until 2000, from where she was reporting on the Kosovo conflict. In 2000 she was in Moscow reporting on big stories like the Kursk submarine tragedy and then it was off to the Middle East. She has never simply read out official statements from governments or terrorists: Guerin's style is to interview the pregnant woman whose house has just been bombed, the doctor who has run out of morphine, or anyone she has met along the way who has a story to tell. 'I've found that people can relate to the individual stories, such as the mother who loses a child or the family that is grieving,' she explains.

There's something about the Irish accent and the way she is obviously not out to impress that makes her intensely credible as a reporter. 'You . . . have to be very dedicated to getting it right, you must make absolutely sure your stories are reliable and that people feel they can believe what you're telling them because credibility is something you can only lose once.'

It may also explain her grim determination to get to the truth, no matter what it takes. A CNN colleague acknowledges that 'she never lets a border check stop her'. She agrees: 'Someone once gave me a very good piece of advice when I was starting out, it may sound very obvious but it was "don't take no for an answer".'

There was controversy when she was moved from the Middle East posting in 2005 after the Israelis complained that she had a pro-Palestinian bias. The Beeb said she had been due for a move anyway and sent her to South Africa, and then on to Pakistan, from where she makes forays across the border into Afghanistan – hardly a soft option for a journalist. You get the impression that Guerin would scoff at soft options. Her husband Michael Georgy was a Reuters correspondent in Baghdad for years after they married, so plenty to discuss at that dinner table after a day at the office . . .

Guerin hasn't lived in Ireland for over twenty years now but says she has 'very, very strong links there' and goes back regularly to visit family or for holidays. She may have become the trusted voice of the British Broadcasting Corporation but for us she is an Irish export who continues to impress every time her face appears on the screen.

*   *   *

Ireland was somewhat shielded from the Second World War. A couple of stray bombs were dropped on Dublin as Messerschmitts got lost or accidentally jettisoned leftover cargo on top of us on the way home. We had wartime rationing but we didn't have the air raid sirens, nights in bomb shelters, death and destruction that our British cousins did. It was intensely political for De Valera to declare neutrality – he had, as they say, 'an agenda' – but I suspect most Irish people felt they were 'neutral on the side of the Allies'. Had a British pilot been shot down over Limerick, an Irishman wouldn't have turned his back, but the same might not be said of a German. There are certainly some now who feel we should have played our part in defeating Nazism, and that neutrality was cowardly.

I think it's fair game that the two countries comment on each other's politics, though. They are near neighbours who speak the same language and their actions can directly affect each other. As well as Orla Guerin, the Irish have given Britain the esteemed BBC journalist Fergal Keane, who only missed having a profile in this book by a whisker by dint of being born in London.

If it's tricky to name Irish folk who had an influence on the British political system, it's also hard to think of influential artists . . . apart from one giant figure of the twentieth century. Know who I'm talking about? You'll find out in the next chapter.

5

THE ARTISTS

THERE'S SOMETHING ABOUT the Irish landscape that encourages creativity. Maybe it's the glorious colours and the incomparable light; maybe it's the fact that it rains so much the Irish need to find activities they can do indoors. British-born artists have always been drawn to the melancholic Dublin autumn or the mesmerizing menace of the Twelve Pins to paint, sculpt, weave, take photos, knit, throw pots – you name it. Every Irish village has at least one resident artist, and they get thicker on the ground the further west you go, until you're tripping over them in the streets of Galway town or out on the islands. It's only fair that we have now sent a few of our home-grown artists over to Britain, where they can benefit from the teaching at British art schools with the prestigious 'royal' prefix, the bulging wallets of British art collectors, and the huge market for designer goods and luxury items in London in particular.

Whereas Irish writers and musicians have always been famous the world over, you may get stuck if you are asked to name an Irish artist or sculptor because few have achieved fame outside Ireland. One reason is that the Irish didn't have any spare cash to buy art while they were struggling with famine, unemployment and years of rebellion against oppression. Poems and songs can be passed on easily from person to person but art is expensive and not quite so portable. If an artist couldn't build a following at home, it would be far harder to build the confidence (or raise the funds) to try his or her luck in overseas markets. There's one towering exception in the twentieth century, whom I'll reveal in a couple of pages. He's so famous that the British have claimed him as their own (a not uncommon phenomenon!) and you may be surprised to hear he's Dublin-born and -bred. It's another of those 'Who would have known it?' moments.

In the late twentieth century, art became a big money game with fortunes changing hands and influential collectors like Charles Saatchi making reputations overnight, long before he found himself fighting to protect his own. It's now become easier for Irish artists to exhibit in London, where they can attract international attention and command prices with lots of noughts on the end, and why wouldn't they? If that's where the wealthy art buyers are, that's where they should go.

And so, joining the comedians and chat show hosts and all those others seeking a bigger audience and an enhanced bank account, we have (drum roll!) the artists. You may have passed their sculptures on the street, you may have bought their handbags and you very likely saw their clothes on royal shoulders. What I'd like to point out now is that in so doing, you are buying Irish.

JOHN HENRY FOLEY: sculptor extraordinaire

24 May 1818–27 August 1874

He abandoned strict academic Neo-classicism and moved towards realism – particularly in creating lively portrait monuments of historical figures.

– John T. Turpin

If you live in or have ever visited the wonderful cities of Dublin or London, the chances are that you have passed a piece of work sculpted by John Henry Foley. The iconic statues of Daniel O'Connell (on O'Connell Street) and of Prince Albert in the Albert Memorial (Kensington Gardens) were brought to the world by this largely uncelebrated Dubliner.

Born in what used to be Dublin's Montgomery Street, Foley was educated at the Royal Dublin Society's art school and the Royal Academy, London. He exhibited at the Royal Academy for the first time in 1839 and commissions were soon pouring in from all over the British Empire for his sculpted figures that were seen as very modern and natural, with relaxed, lifelike postures.

I'm not sure whether Daniel O'Connell, the great campaigner for Catholic emancipation and Irish independence, ever met Prince Albert, consort to Queen Victoria, in real life but their statues regarded each other across Foley's studio because he was working on both at the same time. At forty feet tall, O'Connell would have looked down on the fourteen-foot gilt-bronze figure of Prince Albert that forms the centrepiece of the Albert Memorial. Seated under a grand canopy, Albert is dressed in Garter robes and in one hand he holds the Great Exhibition handbook. O'Connell now stands proudly at the start of Dublin's main thoroughfare, with a relief of fifty figures led by Erin and four Winged Victories.

Foley is most famous for these two, but he also created statues of Lord Clyde in Glasgow, General Stonewall Jackson in Richmond, Virginia, Oliver Goldsmith and Edmund Burke for Trinity College Dublin, Michael Faraday and John Stuart Mill in London, and Sir James Outram for Calcutta. All the bigwigs of the day wanted nothing more than to be cast in bronze in Foley's studio. It was their equivalent of the Hollywood Walk of Fame.

Foley died and was buried in 1874 in the crypt of London's St Paul's Cathedral. However, after Irish independence was achieved in 1921, some saw him as a collaborator with the British Empire and several of his Irish works were damaged or destroyed. The IRA blew up his statue of Lord Gough in Phoenix Park and his statue of Lord Dunkellin in Galway was beheaded and dumped in a river.

The pendulum later swung the other way, though, and his reputation was revived to the extent that Montgomery Street in Dublin, where Foley was born, has now been renamed Foley Street. Ireland doesn't have an honours list but if you get a street named after you, the feeling is that you have done just fine. He is recognized in London as well, where visitors to the Victoria & Albert Museum need only cast their eyes skywards and among the many figures rendered in stone above the windows, they will see a moustachioed figure with his arms across his chest. Beneath this statue is the name, John H. Foley.

FRANCIS BACON: master of the macabre

28 October 1909–28 April 1992

> That man who paints those dreadful pictures.
> – Margaret Thatcher

He's not everyone's cup of tea, with his unsettling bloody carcasses, screaming popes and distorted, writhing figures, but who cares what Mrs Thatcher thought? Few critics deny that he is a towering figure in the history of twentieth-century art.

Francis Bacon would have comfortably slotted into the hell-raisers chapter because he was a notoriously obstreperous boozer, a denizen of Soho's Colony Club along with fellow artists Lucian Freud and Frank Auerbach, a friend to gangsters, a gambler, and a practising homosexual in the days when homosexuality was illegal in London. But really he belongs in this chapter, as one of the greatest artists Ireland has ever produced.

Bacon's father was a racehorse owner with a fondness for drink, and the family was well-off, owning homes in Dublin, Kilcullen, County Kildare, and London, between which he frequently moved around as a child. He didn't receive much formal schooling because of his debilitating asthma but was taught by private tutors. After he left home, his mother set up a trust fund that allowed him to survive when he moved to London, then Berlin and Paris, and there were also some wealthy older lovers to help with the bills.

Bacon didn't have any formal training as an artist and began his professional life as an interior designer but he always enjoyed painting. *Crucifixion* in 1933 was the first of his works to attract attention from the art world, but it was *Three Studies for Figures at the Base of a Crucifixion* in 1945 that really brought him widespread renown, with its strange half-human, half-animal forms and trademark grimness. His work is about the corruption and baseness of humanity and he subverts the artistic conventions of church art by using triptychs and altarpieces to show man as evil and angst-ridden. He always claimed he didn't set out to shock, saying, 'You can't be more horrific than life itself.'

By the late 1980s, his paintings were selling for millions; a triptych went for a record $6 million in 1989, making him the world's most expensive living artist at the time. He didn't favour the trappings of wealth, working in a confined basement in Kensington and producing handfuls of crumpled notes from his pocket to pay the bar bills for himself and his circle of hangers-on. All the major world galleries jostled to own Bacon paintings, but he didn't adopt any airs and graces, sticking with the same group of loyal friends and drinking buddies.

Bacon didn't promote himself as an 'Irish artist' and many wouldn't even have known he was Irish because he had an upper-class English accent and made his home in London. But there is a distinct Irishness in his subversion of Catholicism, his emphasis on the grotesqueness of the body, and the sheer bloody 'life is a struggle' nature of his work. Psychobabble might allow me to suggest the presence of Catholic guilt. Most Irish people over forty claim to suffer from such a thing and it's all tied in with the body, sex, and the attitudes and teachings of the Church in relation to such matters. Back in the 20s, Bacon's father ordered a groom to horsewhip the teenage Francis for being effeminate, and homosexuality was only decriminalized in Ireland in 1996, which should give you an indication of where we stood as a country on what were long considered contentious moral matters. In my opinion, Bacon's contortions of crucifixes and angst add a very Irish twist to the British artistic landscape – and those who claim him as a British artist are just plain wrong.

THE QUIET MEN: portraying immigrant lives

My pictures are comments on the transformation of Irish values over the past thirty or so years. Some of them are also attempts to remember and record those painful aspects of life that we have sought to suppress in our dash for modernity.

– Bernard Canavan

In 2009, a touring exhibition called *The Quiet Men* featured the paintings of five Irish artists, all of them in different ways reflecting the experience of Irish immigrants in Britain over the second half of the twentieth century. You see men queuing for buses, doing their washing in launderettes, drinking in pubs with raised glasses, singing in a corner – or, in the darker pictures, lying in a gutter. They are lonely, brave and proud men trudging a difficult path, with nary a wife or child around.

Three of the five artists in the exhibition had trudged that path themselves, as they were born in Ireland and emigrated to London – Bernard Canavan from County Longford, Danny Carmody from Galway and Dermot Holland from Dublin. The other two – Brian Whelan and John Duffin – were the children of Irish immigrants. They are all of an age to remember the anti-Irish prejudice of the 50s and 60s and well aware of the brutal lives many led in those days when it was hard to get anything but labouring work, meaning they could only afford to live in down-at-heel bedsits with absolutely no mod cons.

Bernard Canavan came to London in the 1950s as soon as he left school and worked in a range of menial jobs before striking lucky when his pictures were chosen for use on London Underground publications in the 1960s. He then went to university to study politics, philosophy and economics and now combines painting with teaching, so his is an emphatic emigration success story. His works are full of emotion without being stereotypical or nostalgic; these are recognizably Irish people dealing with the challenges life throws at them.

Dermot Holland came over at the age of twenty-one and built his reputation bit by bit. His paintings are of ordinary people carrying out the tasks of everyday life: 'not glamorous, but they reflected the experience that we were all living'. It was a subject that hadn't been painted before, and he said he wasn't aiming for high art but something people could identify with.

Of them all, Danny Carmody was recognized by the others as being the most troubled. He came to London in the mid-1970s after his mother's suicide. Settling in Camden, he took work as a bricklayer and began what would be an ongoing battle with alcoholism that saw him in and out of clinics over the next decades, yet at the same time he created more than five hundred huge, brilliant and disturbing paintings – much darker than the work of the other four Quiet Men. The paintings were found by his son in a garage after he took his own life in 2004, and included in the group exhibition he would never see. According to Brian Whelan, 'Danny Carmody was an angry angry man who wore his wounds on his sleeve; yet he captured, most authentically, what it is to be Irish and living in London today.'

I've included them in the book because although not household names (as yet), their work is important in documenting a certain period in the history of Anglo-Irish relations. One that has fortunately passed into the realms of history . . . Just a few decades later, some of our creative émigrés were able to take a much faster, smoother track to success.

PHILIP TREACY: royal hat man

Born 26 May 1967

Give Philip a needle and a thread and he writes a poem.
Give Philip a feather and he writes a song.
– Gianni Versace

Disproving the case that all hatters are mad, Philip Treacy graduated from playing with his sister's dolls to designing headgear for duchesses (Cornwall) and ladies (Gaga).

Born in the small rural village of Ahascragh, County Galway, young Philip loved to watch weddings, which he saw as a local form of fashion show. By the age of five he was making dresses and hats for his sister's dolls, breaking the rules by sneaking on to his mother's sewing machine while she was out the back feeding chickens. After leaving school he travelled across the country to study fashion at the National College of Art and Design in Dublin and began making hats as a sideline, just to finish off his outfits. He did well and was lucky enough to win a place on the MA course at the Royal College of Art in London.

Treacy's big break came in 1989 when *Tatler* style editor Isabella Blow asked him to design her wedding hat. She explained, 'I'd rather spend the money on his hats than on plastic surgery any day! He's saving us from the scalpel.' Within a year he was designing for Chanel and Karl Lagerfeld, then he opened his own shop and quickly became the most sought-after milliner of his generation.

There are some who mock. People were very cruel about the loopy fascinator Princess Beatrice wore to Kate and William's wedding in 2011, saying it looked like a toilet seat. And the jury is still out on the telephone hat that Lady Gaga wore on the Jonathan Ross show in 2010. But he remains the go-to man when Sarah Jessica Parker wants something different to wear to a film premiere or the Harry Potter crew need some wacky new hats for their wizards.

In 2007 Treacy accepted an OBE from the Queen – one of many in this book to do so. Pre-peace process, there might have been those who would have accused him of taking the 'Queen's shilling' and her ribbon with a bottle top attached as well, while subjugated on bended knee. Now we just think it's nice for people who have done well to get some recognition. Gotta grab the gongs where you can since we still don't have an honours system back in Ireland, more's the pity.

PAUL COSTELLOE: the princesses' choice
Born June 1945

[Irish women are] only a couple of generations out of the bog . . . [They] wouldn't know style if it tottered up to them in 10-inch heels.

Paul Costelloe got himself into a huge heap of trouble with his provocative statement about Irish women's lack of style, but he's a maverick with a cheeky grin and a twinkle in his eye who didn't mind a bit. 'It made me from being a designer to being a bit of a celebrity – so it was worth the pain,' he chuckles.

Paul's father was from Limerick and his mother from New York so there's a transatlantic vibe. He went to the same school as me – Blackrock College in Dublin – but about twenty years earlier, so our paths didn't cross in the hallowed corridors. He moved to Paris in the late 1960s and trained in the couture houses there before heading to Italy, back to Dublin, and finally relocating to London in 1999 when he was already pretty successful. Princess Diana loved his dresses and invited him to Kensington Palace to sketch designs for her overseas trips. Diana's daughter-in-law Kate has already been seen in Costelloe couture, so she's carrying on the royal first-lady tradition.

I met Paul when he came on the *Late Late Show* in 2011. A big, tall guy, he's very commanding in appearance. He was wearing a flouncy shirt but you could tell there was lots of testosterone floating around the place. You wouldn't expect someone quite so masculine to work in the fashion industry, but there it is. On that show, Paul got into a heated debate with comedian Neil Delamere about the royal wedding, which had just been shown wall-to-wall on Irish TV. Neil cracked a joke about Kate Middleton hardly being the 'commoner' the media kept reporting her to be, with her private schooling and millionaire parents. Paul argued robustly that her parents were self-made and that her school fees had been paid by her solicitor grandfather. He rejected any implication that the event was vulgar, insisting he just liked 'seeing people doing things well, in good taste'.

What was interesting to me was that, in a real sign of the times, the studio audience seemed to be firmly behind Paul and supportive of the royals. We got a few complaints afterwards – but only about what Neil had said. For me, the reaction to that wedding in Ireland showed a significant sea change in attitudes. Those who had watched Charles and Diana's 1981 wedding with the curtains firmly closed and the sound turned down for fear of neighbours catching them out could now openly admit to having watched Kate and William. And why not?

ORLA KIELY: the queen of prints

Born 1964

It was lovely . . . the greens, the yellows . . . the clouds, the skies and the sea. In a sense it's not colourful, but you do see accents in the wild flowers by the road, or the yellow gorse on the mountains.

– Orla Kiely on her Irish childhood

Of all the recent badges of honour for the Irish and British middle classes, none is more instantly recognizable than the designs of Dubliner Orla Kiely. The distinctive patterns that separate her products from the rest were inspired by her childhood home in the 60s and 70s, where her mother had 'olive green Formica cupboards and a gloss orange ceiling . . . I still like the idea of a mad ceiling.' She was also inspired by leafy walks in the rural hills near her Dublin home. Her colours are autumnal and Ireland is pretty much constantly autumnal. We never get cold to the point of freezing or hot to the point we feel like we're melting away. In my opinion her palette is a particularly Irish one.

Having completed an MA in knitwear at the Royal College of Art in London – that useful 'royal' prefix at work again – Kiely went to New York to study wallpaper and fabric design and on her return went into business making hats with her husband Dermott Rowan. It was an unlikely but critical intervention by Kiely's father at London Fashion Week that helped shift her career in the right direction. As he was visiting his daughter's small stand, Mr Kiely observed that no one was wearing hats any more but that everyone was carrying a bag. With that advice, the designer changed her course – and headed for global domination.

Just as the world went crazy for black and white, Orla Kiely introduced her colourful Stem designs and they started appearing on everything from laminated handbags to tablecloths. The trademark repeated motif reflects the designer's thought process, she says: 'I sometimes think that my brain works in repeat. I love the order and regiment of repetition and how everything can be patterned in this way, as if you are looking at the world through a prism or a kaleidoscope.' There's a nostalgic feel about her patterns that ties in neatly with the modern craze for vintage.

As Kiely branched out into clothing design, so too did her fan base. In the summer of 2012, Pippa Middleton, the world's most famous sister-in-law, sat in the royal box at Ascot resplendent in an elegant Kiely navy dress and buttoned-up macramé jacket, and glamorous granny Carole Middleton wore a Kiely dress to visit new baby George in hospital. You can now buy Orla Kiely water bottles, furniture, wallpaper, kitchenware, stationery – and even a Citroën 2CV in Kiely colours and patterns!

The designer has accepted an OBE for services to the British fashion industry – and she's popular in Ireland as well, making her a real Anglo-Irish success story. But I still come across people in Britain who don't know how to pronounce her surname, so just for the record it sounds the same as the first name of the diminutive Australian pop singer whose surname is Minogue.

PAURIC SWEENEY: the bag man
Born 1973

Fashion cannot and must not be an absolute idea; it morphs and evolves as society changes.

I knew Pauric Sweeney back when we were both in the same maths class at Blackrock College – the one for people who weren't any good at maths. We also attended the same Irish class – for people who were no good at Irish. But none of this held him back from a meteoric rise to fame, with only a slight detour along the way.

Pauric was born in Donegal, schooled in Dublin and then flew out to Philadelphia to study architecture. Fashion had always interested him, and he began designing jewellery first of all. He came to London in 1998 just as the young Brit Art bunch – Tracey Emin, Damien Hirst, the Chapman Brothers – were banking their first millions, and he settled in the east of London where all the buzz was happening. It was September 2000 when his first clothing collection 'Wish U Were Gothic' launched in Paris and he was soon attracting a celebrity clientele, with Madonna said to be a big fan of his velour tracksuits.

It was 2005 when Pauric launched his first range of bags, the accessory for which he is now most famous. Givenchy and Christian Lacroix came knocking, and success was assured. His gold python overnight bag or the pistachio-green alligator one: how to choose? You can see the architectural influence in the flowing shapes and innovative styles but it's not as if he was following in the footsteps of anyone from back home. 'Creatively, Ireland developed an ability to pass on history, to tell stories,' he says. 'It's very open; very expressive. But no big handbag history, no.'

He's now moved his workshop to Italy to work with Italian tanners, but jets round the world on a breathtaking schedule, from London to Tokyo and New York to Dublin in the time you and I might take to do the weekly supermarket shop.

Unlike many of the others in this book, Pauric has made Anglo-Irish success look easy. If you haven't heard of him yet, you're just not a Class A fashionista.

*　　*　　*

At last, Irish artists have found a way to get a break in the British market and use it as a springboard to international success. Each of the ones I've featured here brings their own distinctive Irish vision and their unique subject matter. Before you write in, I know there are hundreds of other great Irish artists, many of whom have lived in the UK, but I'm not writing an encyclopedia so save your breath. This is my take on some of the major artists and designers who crossed the water and as such I stand by it.

You'd better get used to me just including my own favourites because the next chapter, about writers, could be a book in itself if I were so inclined. But as in the rest of the book, I'll stick to my own selection methods, with decisions made and ratified by a committee of one. Me.

6
THE WRITERS

ONE OF THE GREAT clichés about Ireland is that it's the Land of Saints and Scholars. The saints we'll leave to the theologians but here we're going to dwell on the scholars: the pen-wielding, keyboard-clicking, coffee-quaffing wordsmiths who took themselves out of Ireland but never quite managed to take Ireland out of themselves.

Ireland can have that effect on writers in particular. When you look at the men and women writers who made Britain their home, most of them are defined by their Irishness. It's a visceral thing in many respects and very hard to shake. I have a particular love of Connemara in the west of Ireland. In Cromwell's time, the threat was that enemies would be sent 'to Hell or to Connaught' (the province farthest west), such was the remote and barren nature of the place, and yet every couple of months I feel the need to get back there even for just a couple of nights. It feeds the soul and, helpfully, the Guinness there is particularly creamy. So I think I can imagine what a writer must be going through when they leave the beauty of Leenane for the hullabaloo of London. For many of the writers discussed in this chapter, Ireland has remained a muse long after emigration. A muse *in absentia*, but a muse nonetheless.

Throw a stone in Ireland and you'll hit a writer – and not just a wannabe one like myself. I'm talking about world-class authors who have chosen not to emigrate. Seamus Heaney, Colm Tóibín, John Banville, Roddy Doyle, Patrick McCabe and Conor McPherson are just a few. When the Booker Prize longlist was announced in 2013, three of the thirteen authors were Irish (Colm Tóibín, Colum McCann and Donal Ryan) and all three very much deserved their place there. Colm Tóibín has ended up on the shortlist. What other country of Ireland's size can boast such literary endeavour? With the world shrinking by way of technology and budget flights, there's no need to come to Britain to find your audience. The written word travels very quickly and easily in the twenty-first century. But for Irish writers who do cross the water, that word is still – and always has been – infused with a twist of home.

JONATHAN SWIFT: the godfather of satire

30 November 1667–19 October 1745

> Satire is a sort of glass, wherein beholders do generally discover everybody's face but their own.
>
> – *The Battle of the Books*

There's something very Irish about satire: the insult masquerading as a compliment. As a people, we tend to be allergic to pretentiousness and cynical about those in positions of authority – themes that recur time and again in Swift's works.

Swift was born in Dublin to Protestant parents and attended Trinity College before deciding on a career in the Church. He became dean of St Patrick's Cathedral, a beautiful building in the heart of Dublin. He hoped to get a position in England where he could advance his Church career, but in fact it was as a writer of political pamphlets that he began to make his name in London. (These were the days when the political pamphlet was hugely influential and read by recipients as opposed to now when they go from doormat to green bin within seconds.) His first major satire was *The Battle of the Books* (1704) in which he imagines books in a library arguing over whether ancient or modern learning is superior. That was followed by *A Tale of a Tub* (1704), in which he tells the story of the Catholic Church, the Church of England and Non-Conformism as three quarrelling brothers, full of self-glorification. And then there was *A Modest Proposal* (1729) in which he suggests that the Irish poor should sell their babies as food to the rich. He'd probably get elected in Ireland today on the strength of that proposal alone . . . Anyway, you get the way the man's mind worked.

In 1726 Swift published *Gulliver's Travels*, the book for which he's most famous today. You can read this simply as a story of a man shipwrecked among little people, the Lilliputians – that's what Hollywood has always done (both Richard Harris and Chris O'Dowd have starred in big-screen versions). But on closer inspection, it's an intricate satire of the English, the Church, the politics of the day, scientists, and ultimately humanity itself: 'I cannot but conclude the bulk of your natives to be the most pernicious race of little odious vermin that nature ever suffered to crawl upon the surface of the earth.'

You get the impression Swift can't have been easy to live with, what with all the anger issues – and he certainly had his fair share of enemies in both Church and state – but inside his works there is the beating heart of humanity. Irish humanity.

BRAM STOKER: the blood-sucker

8 November 1847–20 April 1912

My revenge is just begun! I spread it over
centuries, and time is on my side.

> – *Dracula*

Drac O'la anyone? OK, the Count himself is Transylvanian but his creator was from Clontarf, Dublin, and some of the influences for his most famous story came from the annals of Irish history. As a child Stoker was sickly and frequently bedridden and his mother entertained him by telling tales from her own Sligo childhood, tales of supernatural happenings and bloodthirsty deaths. The Stokers could trace their ancestry back to Manus the Magnificent, a warrior who once ruled all of Ireland and had the power of life and death over his serfs, which could well be the inspiration for Count Dracula, who says in the 1897 novel, 'I myself am of an old family.'

The story-telling techniques used by Stoker are reminiscent of those used by the Seanchaí in ancient times. He was the servant to the clan chief who kept track of important traditions and told stories of Finn mac Cumhail, the mythical giant whose wife was turned into a deer, or of leprechauns and the dangers of straying into fairy rings. Seanchaí is a word we still use to refer to the guy who sits down to tell a story and everyone stops to listen for five minutes or however long it takes – in pubs, or by the flickering firelight in someone's home. Often they are spooky stories that make chills run up and down the spines of the rapt audience.

Stoker studied at University College Dublin and an interest in theatre led him to become the drama critic for the Dublin *Evening Mail*. After he gave a favourable review to the great Henry Irving's Hamlet at the Theatre Royal, he received an invitation to dinner and the two became firm friends. In 1878 he married a famous beauty, Florence Balcombe, one of whose exes was Oscar Wilde – I can't imagine Oscar was too bereft at this loss – and started moving in fashionable circles. Stoker's first Gothic-style novel *The Snake's Pass* was published in 1890 to much acclaim.

Spiritualism was popular at the time and he was friendly with Sherlock Holmes's creator Arthur Conan Doyle, who later became a prominent advocate of séances and the afterlife. Stoker himself joined a bizarre magic order called the Golden Dawn, where they taught weird but very trendy phenomena like astral travel and geomancy. Add to this a meeting with a Hungarian writer called Ármin Vámbéry, who told him some myths and legends of the Carpathian Mountains, and you can begin to see where Stoker got the idea for Dracula, his most famous creation, the one that was to secure his place in history.

Nowadays, we're more familiar with the various big- and small-screen incarnations of the Transylvanian count. The first was Friedrich Wilhelm Murnau's *Nosferatu* in 1922; fast forward through several versions to the British Hammer Horror films of the 1950s to the 1970s, in which Christopher Lee played a high-camp Count Dracula with staring eyes and blood dripping down his chin; then there was Tom Cruise in *Interview with a Vampire*, followed by *Buffy* and *Twilight*, and even the current literary sensation *50 Shades of Grey* is a spin-off, one that could never hold a candle to the brilliance that was *Sesame Street*'s Count. Whatever would Mr Stoker have thought?

OSCAR WILDE: the witty aesthete

16 October 1854–30 November 1900

There is no sin except stupidity.
– 'The Critic as Artist'

Oscar Fingal O'Flahertie Wills Wilde was a man of contradictions: he lived in England and was in many ways anglophile yet he supported Home Rule for Ireland; he was Protestant with strong leanings towards the Catholic Church; he was a hugely successful writer who professed to find writing boring; a relentless self-publicist who did his best to hide his true nature; and a married father of two who was homosexual. It must have been tough being Oscar.

His background was comfortable enough: a middle-class upbringing in a Georgian house in Dublin's Merrion Square with an eye surgeon father and a mother who ran literary salons. He flourished at Trinity College Dublin and at Oxford, then began to dabble with writing, publishing his own volume of poems – in three editions so it would look as though it had been so successful he'd had to reprint. He did a tour of the United States, lecturing on the Aesthetic Movement and living the good life (his capacity for alcohol was apparently legendary), then on his return he got married and became editor of *Woman's World* magazine to earn a living. From 1888 to 1895, he wrote non-stop and all his best works appeared: *The Happy Prince*, *The Picture of Dorian Gray*, *Lady Windermere's Fan*, *The Importance of Being Earnest* . . . He enjoyed satirizing English pretension in characters like the famous Lady Bracknell, to whom he gave classic lines such as 'To lose one parent may be regarded as a misfortune; to lose both looks like carelessness.' The truth is, I could fill the next ten pages with Wildean wit, such was his capacity for cutting cleverness, but we must get back to his story . . .

At the height of his success, Wilde was a tortured soul because from 1891 he was madly in love with a man – Alfred Douglas, third son of the 9th Marquess of Queensberry. They had a passionate and not particularly secret affair which, Wilde wrote to Douglas, 'was like feasting with panthers; the danger was half the excitement'. Homosexuality was strictly illegal, and Wilde was an establishment figure with plays on all over the West End. Douglas was not very subtle in his affections and soon it was the talk of London. Still nothing might have happened if Wilde hadn't decided to sue Douglas's father for a note he left at Oscar's club accusing him of sodomy. The court case was a fiasco, which ended with Oscar being charged with gross indecency. The whole house of cards collapsed: his plays were taken off the stage and his books removed from bookshops; bailiffs auctioned his possessions; his children were forced to leave the country; and, finally, he was jailed for two years. When he came out, his health had been damaged and he moved to France, where he lived incognito under the name Sebastian Melmoth.

It is one of literature's cruellest tragedies. He was a man born out of his time. Nowadays, Oscar would probably be a chat show host on BBC One or a West End staple with a permanent table at the Ivy – or both. He most certainly would have been fêted and admired rather than dying in poverty far from home.

On his deathbed, Wilde was baptised into the Catholic Church but his last thoughts weren't of God, or family, or Ireland: 'Either that wallpaper goes or I do,' he said just before he expired, an aesthete to the last.

GEORGE BERNARD SHAW:
the opinionated funny man

26 July 1856–2 November 1950

I often quote myself. It adds spice to my conversations.
– *John Bull's Other Island*

You'd think Shaw and Wilde would have been friends: both Dublin-born exiles in London, both playwrights, both witty – but, in fact, whenever they met they felt awkward around each other. They wrote and sent each other copies of their plays, but tried to avoid social encounters. Maybe it was Shaw's ardent socialism that was off-putting. Wilde once said of him, 'he has no enemies but is intensely disliked by all his friends' – a line Shaw was so taken with that he quoted it about himself! But to give him his due, when Wilde was imprisoned, Shaw petitioned the Home Secretary for his early release, and in an era when Wilde's name was taboo, Shaw kept referring to his plays in his drama criticism.

Shaw's company may have been a little dull for the lively Oscar Wilde, but his work was renowned. As far as I know, G. B. Shaw is the only person to have been awarded both a Nobel Prize (1925) and an Oscar (1938) – quite the mantelpiece display. He was prolific, writing more than sixty plays, as well as essays, criticism, short stories, novels – and he was funny. In 1904, King Edward VII laughed so hard at the play *John Bull's Other Island* at the Royal Court Theatre that he broke his seat.

Shaw was born in Dublin's Upper Synge Street to a mother who was a mezzo-soprano and a father who was a heavy drinker. When he was sixteen, his mother left to pursue her singing career in

133

London and Shaw followed four years later, which is when he began writing full-time. He was converted simultaneously to socialism and vegetarianism and joined the then-influential Fabian Society, for whom he wrote pamphlets and gave speeches. He also became theatre critic for the *Pall Mall Gazette*, under the pen name Cornoo di Bassetto (nothing too clever – it simply means basset horn!) and savaged productions he didn't like, with Sir Henry Irving coming in for a particular mauling: 'He does not merely cut plays; he disembowels them.'

It is for his own plays that Shaw is best remembered, and many are still revived in the twenty-first century: *Arms and the Man*, *Pygmalion* (which became the musical *My Fair Lady*), *Man and Superman*, *Saint Joan*, *Major Barbara*. He was embraced at the heart of the British establishment until 1914, when his popularity suffered after publication of his Swiftian manifesto 'Common Sense about the War', in which he suggested soldiers in all armies should shoot their officers. Not ideal in the year Britain declared war on Germany. He was not a supporter of the Irish Free State, but he campaigned against the execution of leaders of the 1916 Uprising and invited Michael Collins for dinner at his home.

Shaw was a man of strong opinions and if he got it wrong sometimes – with his support for Stalin and his interest in eugenics – at least he made people laugh. He was a household name in both Britain and Ireland in his own lifetime for his ironic humour, which became known as 'Shavian wit': 'My way of joking is to tell the truth,' he quipped. 'It's the funniest joke in the world.'

EDNA O'BRIEN: the country girl

Born 15 December 1930

> When anyone asks me about the Irish character, I say look at the trees. Maimed, stark and misshapen, but ferociously tenacious.

Edna O'Brien is an elegant, erudite woman who's always taken a wry look back at Irish society since she moved over to Britain at the age of twenty-four. I've interviewed her on the *Late Late Show* and she was a wonderful interviewee with a distinctively Irish way about her. She may have left Ireland over fifty years ago but Ireland certainly never left her and I'm sure it never will.

O'Brien grew up in Tuamgraney in County Clare, about which she says, 'A writer's life commences in childhood; all one's associations and feelings are steeped in it.' It was a troubled childhood, with a violent unpredictable father, and when she had the chance to escape to London through marriage to a man her parents disapproved of, she grabbed it and escaped, relieved.

'Exile and separation were very, very good for me,' says the grande dame. 'If I'd stayed in Ireland, I might not have had the inner strength to carry on writing.' She was astonished by the reaction back home to her first novel *The Country Girls* in 1960. It's a coming-of-age tale of two girls, one who wants to be a poet and the other who wants to marry a rich man, and – hold the front page! – it describes their sexual experiences. It was shocking and horrific to many at the time because, as one wag said later, there was no sex in Ireland before the *Late Late Show*. O'Brien was treated 'like a Jezebel' when she went to visit her mother after publication, and all the neighbours' curtains were twitching. The book was banned, burned and denounced at the pulpit. Understandably, she was happy to escape back to London again and the party set she hung out with in leafy SW20.

Fortunately for us, she carried on writing, although she did get herself into hot water again with books like *Girls in their Married Bliss* (1964) and *August is a Wicked Month* (1965). One of her recurring themes is the subordination of women. During her up-bringing men were always separate from women; couples never sat together in church or held hands in the street, and men were distant, domineering figures. Once she started writing, she realized that it was hard to be taken as seriously as male writers and wrote of the difficulty of being a woman in what was still ostensibly a man's world. She was the first truly successful Irish woman novelist so there was an important trail to blaze – and fortunately she was up to the challenge.

It must be an odd feeling to be an émigré who only ever returns for short periods, and she admits, 'The two countries have warred within me.' But it seems to me she couldn't have become the writer – and the woman – she became without making that move. She wouldn't have met R. D. Laing and taken the LSD trip that she claims deepened the darkness within her and thus deepened her writing. She wouldn't have partied with all the happening young people of the 1960s (actors, writers, politicians, musicians – you name them, they probably turned up at one of her Saturday night parties). And she wouldn't have rebelled properly against the strict Catholic schooling and the hypocrisy of Catholicism as it was taught in a country where not only *Country Girls* but her next six books were banned.

I think Edna O'Brien is a classic example of the type of Irish person who needed to travel to a bigger room in order to look back on the small room of Ireland effectively. According to fellow Irish novelist Colum McCann, she has been 'the advance scout for the Irish imagination' – and as far as I'm concerned, she's done it with impeccable style.

MARIAN KEYES: any craic?
Born 10 September 1963

> What doesn't kill us makes us funnier.
> – *The Other Side of the Story*

Marian Keyes is a sprightly, lively, loquacious woman. She's a great person to interview on television: I don't really have to earn my money that night because I can just sit back and let her off. She sees life through a prism of humour but there are heavy emotional undertones amidst the laughter. All her readers appreciate her honesty when she talks about the crippling depression that has afflicted her over the years and that nearly led her to take her own life in 2010.

Marian was born in Limerick and grew up in a household where there was always a lot of story-telling, in finest Seanchaí tradition. After school she studied law at Dublin University then moved to London for work and didn't pick up a pen until she was in her thirties. In 1995 she showed some short stories to a publisher, they wanted to see a novel and so she quickly penned *Watermelon*, her first best-seller. Readers on both sides of the Irish Sea loved the quirky Irish humour and her universal language of modern womanhood.

More best-sellers followed – *Lucy Sullivan is Getting Married* (1996), *This Charming Man* (2008), *The Mystery of Mercy Close* (2012) – and she won at the Irish Book Awards in 2009. Her themes are often dark ones, of domestic abuse and alcoholism, but there is a strong central female character who survives in the end. She's very much in the tradition of Irish doyenne the late Maeve Binchy with her interest in human nature and her compulsive, addictive books that leave readers clamouring for the next.

Marian hit fifty in September 2013 and she took my call on the radio that morning. She said she'd had a lovely time with her family but went onto describe the painful effects of depression that she has been dealing with in recent times. In a raw but honest conversation, Marian said that on a bad day she can't get out of bed but that she has accepted her lot and that eases the burden. Throughout our exchange, the trademark mischief was present but the honesty about her illness was as disarming as it was impressive.

Naturally hilarious, someone once called her '*Sex in the City* meets Mrs Doyle from *Father Ted*'. Here's her on her height: 'I never wear flats. My shoes are so high that sometimes when I step out of them, people look around in confusion and ask, "Where'd you go?" and I have to say 'I'm down here!"' She's found new fans through social media and through her appearances on Britain's *Strictly Come Dancing*, and I for one am delighted by her success.

*   *   *

Yes, I know I've missed out dozens of great Irish wordsmiths – but I did warn you. It's impossible to sum up the huge contribution the Irish have made to literature written in the English language. We've even added some of our own words to it. There's 'hooligan', which can be traced back to the 1890s and may derive from the Irish surname Ó'hUallacháin (which became Houlihan or Hoolohan). A popular music-hall song back then featured a fictional rowdy Irish family called the Hooligans and before long, the word crossed the Irish Sea and entered the hallowed pages of the *Oxford English Dictionary* as 'a violent young troublemaker, typically one of a gang'. Not something the Irish specially want to be known for.

Another word the British adopted is, believe it or not, 'Tory'. This comes from the Irish word *tóir*, which means 'to pursue', and referred to Irish highwaymen whose land had been snatched by English settlers. When the Catholic King James II was being excluded from the succession, his supporters were labelled 'tories' as a derogatory term but the word was later adopted by the Conservative party as a badge of honour, and remains in use today. You're welcome, Great Britain!

And there's another story behind the word 'boycott'. This came from Captain Charles Boycott, who was a land agent in County Mayo responsible for evicting tenants who weren't keeping up with the rent increases. So unpopular was he that he needed police protection. Labourers refused to work for him, his cattle were scattered and no one would harvest his crops. The word 'boycott' was born and is now defined as 'to withdraw from commercial or social relations with (a country, organization or person) as a punishment or protest'.

The Irish have given the British lots more words, including craic, shenanigans, smithereens – I think you'll agree that they all have a distinctive lilt about them. Of course, they sound better with an Irish accent but we're happy for British friends to come up with their best approximation.

You'll have noticed that a disproportionate number of Irish

writers are playwrights, and there's a reason for this. The Irish love watching their stories acted out for them, whether it's the Seanchaí getting up from his chair to demonstrate, or a full cast on stage at the Abbey Theatre. So my next chapter is all about those people who act out stories for a living: the thespians.

7

THE
THESPIANS

NOT UNLIKE RADIO AND TELEVISION PRESENTERS, actors are vain creatures who like to command the attention of every room they enter. (We're back to the room analogy again because it's particularly pertinent in this chapter.) Despite a most respectable and respected theatrical heritage, Ireland has trouble keeping its finest actors at home because sometimes the room can feel too small and they want a larger space to display their talent. The siren call of London's West End is compelling and the financial rewards substantial. Chances are the London theatres will be bigger and busier, thereby providing the actor with what they want and need most: an audience, ergo attention! Add to that the chances of being seen by a Hollywood producer who might be passing through town and you have a game changer.

The tradition of Irish men and women travelling to the UK for acting work is a long one. There's Charles Macklin (1699–1797), who killed a man in a fight over a wig at the Theatre Royal, Drury Lane; Lola Montez (1821–61), an actress and dancer who became the mistress of Ludwig I of Bavaria; Cyril Cusack (1910–93), who was a leading light at the Royal Shakespeare Company in the 1960s – and many more.

Nowadays, Irish actors have more choice. Instead of chancing their luck on the London stage, they can bypass the UK entirely and go straight to Hollywood for an even bigger audience and an even bigger pay cheque. That was the route taken by Gabriel Byrne, Colin Farrell and Saoirse Ronan, among others. For those who don't go straight to America, the UK can still be a handy stepping-stone to bigger things. And if your main interest is theatre rather than blockbuster movies, London is probably a better bet.

Back in the late 80s and early 90s there was a brief boom in Irish film, with a string of international hits, partly because of the foundation of the Irish Film Board in 1980, which helped to fund new movies. Jim Sheridan was able to make *My Left Foot* (1989), *The Field* (1990) and *In the Name of the Father* (1993). Neil Jordan made *The Crying Game* (1992) and *The Butcher Boy* (1997), among others. Tom Cruise came to Ireland to star in *Far and Away* (1992), Alan Parker was lured over to make *The Commitments* (1991), then Mel Gibson made his William Wallace film *Braveheart* in 1995 (sorry, Scotland!). During this halcyon period it looked as though Irish actors might not have to emigrate to get work after all – but all too soon, this fertile period ended and hasn't been repeated since. Of course, there have been some good Irish films since then (*Adam and Paul*, *Garage* and *What Richard Did* stand out) but not enough to keep all our talented thespians in gainful employment. That's why the Irish export some across to Britain.

In this chapter I'll look at a few Irish actors who chose the British route to stardom. Some of them play Irish and there are others you'd never guess were Irish if I wasn't here to tell you, but all of them have made their own unique contributions to British dramatic art.

WILFRED BRAMBELL: the original grumpy old man

22 March 1912–18 January 1985

> You dirty old man.
> – Harold Steptoe to his father

Falling neatly into the category of 'I didn't know he was Irish' comes a man who remains, in the public imagination at least, a curmudgeonly crank with a bad attitude. As Albert Edward Ladysmith Steptoe, Wilfrid Brambell dominated the rag and bone yard he inhabited with his eternal bachelor son, Harold, whom he irritates to distraction with his filthy habits and sly selfishness.

Steptoe and Son began life as a BBC play, *The Offer*. The viewer response was so favourable that a six-part series was commissioned and duly began broadcasting in June 1962. The public loved the filial friction between the scheming old man and his put-upon son so much that the series ran for twenty-four episodes, not ending until November 1965. *Steptoe and Son* had four further series from 1970 to 1974. I remember the reruns as part of the culture during my childhood when we all cringed at the sheer disgustingness of old man Steptoe.

Brambell was born in Rathgar, a comfortable suburb of Dublin. As a young boy during the First World War, he sang songs for wounded soldiers at the local hospital and thus a life performing in front of audiences began. Brief stints as a journalist and part-time repertory player were followed by tours with the Entertainments National Service Association during the Second World War. Ireland's neutrality in the war obviously wasn't an issue for Brambell, given the chance to get out on stage and make a name.

At the conclusion of that war, Wilfrid made it to the big screen in a Carol Reed thriller *Odd Man Out* (1947). This was the era when most of the Irish in London were navvies so he did well to get plentiful television work, even if he might have grumbled that he was typecast as a grumpy old man long before his big breakthrough came with Steptoe. Pop culture embraced Wilfrid in 1964 when he was cast in *A Hard Day's Night* as Paul McCartney's granddad and he made frequent appearances on stage.

It wasn't all plain sailing, though. Brambell was homosexual, which was utterly taboo in Ireland at the time and even remained illegal in Britain until 1967. In December 1962, he picked up a conviction for 'importuning for an immoral purpose at Shepherd's Bush Green' and was conditionally discharged but ordered to pay 25 guineas in costs. He was also an alcoholic, which meant he frequently forgot his lines and once made a major faux pas on television in New Zealand when the presenter asked him what he thought of the place: 'I hate your fucking cathedrals. I hate your fucking town. It's the lowest place I've been in all my life,' he retorted, generating all kinds of unfavourable headlines.

Like so many great comedy duos, relations between Brambell and his co-star Harry Corbett reportedly deteriorated to the point that they loathed each other, but their fates were linked; both would forever be best known as the son who aspired to a good life of fine wine and parties, and the old man who proudly broke wind and dropped his dentures in his dinner. Maybe not the best advert for Irishness then – unlike my next subject, who is one of Ireland's finest-ever acting exports.

MICHAEL GAMBON: a talent for divilment

Born 19 October 1940

I like being rough around the edges. A big, interesting old bugger.

For a number of years, Michael Gambon would settle himself in the dressing room of whatever theatre he was working in by arranging sentimental items about the place. One of them was a framed photograph of the man himself posing alongside Robert De Niro. Scrawled across the bottom of the photo is a message that reads 'To Mike, best wishes and love forever, Bob.' He claimed this had been given to him during the 1980s when he was respected in theatre circles but unknown internationally so it was quite a trophy to possess. It was the first thing any visitor to his dressing room commented on, such was the wattage of Hollywood's finest and Gambon was more than happy to regale these guests with stories of his time spent with 'Bob'.

The truth of the story is that it's a lie. Gambon hadn't worked with De Niro at that stage and wouldn't do so until 2006. As for the framed photo? He simply got a picture of De Niro from the film *The King of Comedy* and slapped a shot of himself beside it before adding the bon mots. Welcome to Gambonville, a mischievous world where marvellous anecdotes are told – many of which are true, and some of which are decidedly not.

We'll get to more of these later but first let's try to sort out some of the facts. What we do know is that Michael Gambon was born in Dublin in 1940 but that he only lived there until he was five. Or maybe six. But he definitely lived there. He has no memory of his time in Dublin but does recall 'coming back on holidays with my parents, going to the seaside and all that'. The Gambons settled in Camden, a home from home for the hordes of Irish who were fleeing Ireland. Although the Chinese got a 'Town' and the Italians got a 'Little', Ireland got nothing bar a reputation for staying up late and heavy drinking, both of which were interchangeable.

In school Gambon was, like so many performers, a class clown who wanted and enjoyed the attention: 'If you're at school and don't feel very confident, you become the butt of people's jokes, don't you? You play up that side of you to protect yourself. I think that must be what I was.' It was this curious collision of shyness and tomfoolery that would shape the sense of humour and temperament that defined both man and boy.

Gambon parted ways with the education system at fifteen and secured a job as a toolmaker at Vickers Armstrong, where he completed an apprenticeship and developed a lifelong interest in and love of all things mechanical. At the urging of his father, Gambon visited his local theatre where they needed help in set building. However, on the day he walked through the door, they also needed a bit player to appear in a performance that night, albeit as someone simply serving a cup of tea. 'I went, varoom!' he later remembered. 'I thought, Jesus, this is for me. I want to be an actor.' And in that swift but important moment, Michael Gambon's life changed utterly.

By now a movie fan, the aspiring actor set his sights on being the next James Dean but a detour to the Albery Theatre when he was nineteen changed that. At a production of *The Long and the Short and the Tall*, Gambon was mesmerized by the leading actor, his compatriot Peter O'Toole. The lithe, panther-like thespian duly supplanted the hunched-up, eye-narrowing smoker as the actor he most wanted to be like.

Gambon was enjoying his early days as an amateur actor but he felt it was time to move onwards and upwards so he set his sights on his hometown of Dublin and the venerable Gate Theatre. Putting pen to paper he dreamed up a CV and wrote to the man in charge: 'I told him a lot of lies, as you do, because I was of the opinion that people didn't really read letters.' He invented appearances he had made in the West End of London and added (for extra effect) that the only reason he was in Dublin at all was because he was en route to New York. Whatever the quality of the spoof, Gambon secured a small part in a touring production of *Othello*, cast as Second Gentleman of Cyprus. It is entirely possible that the man who ran the Gate Theatre didn't believe the contents of the letter but admired its audacity enough to give this charlatan a part, however small.

It wasn't long before Gambon returned to London, armed with his 'vast' experience as a Shakespearean Cypriot gent. Within a year he joined Laurence Olivier's National Theatre, where his talents were required as a spear-carrier.

Soon thereafter, Gambon and his idol Peter O'Toole shared a stage in a National production of *Hamlet*. Gambon remembers: 'O'Toole had just done *Lawrence of Arabia*. We were all in awe of him, us walk-ons. We'd walk on and stare at him. Stand there with our spears and work our way nearer to him, you know, shuffle across the stage just to get close.' It was close enough for some of the lustre to rub off on Gambon, whose career started to take off.

Throughout the 70s and into the 80s Gambon was earning a reputation as one of the great coming men of British theatre. On stage as Galileo in 1980, his performance elicited such a positive reaction from audience and players alike that he claims he wept with gratitude. Six years later, he was cast as *The Singing Detective* in the Dennis Potter television drama. The universal acclaim led to a slew of offers and he hasn't stopped working since.

Throughout his years on stage, there was always time to indulge himself. After an appearance with Anthony Hopkins on a typical night, Gambon reminisces: 'We'd go to the pub next door to the Vic, then we'd go to the Salisbury up the road. Then we'd go to the Buxton, an actor's club. From the Buxton we'd go to Jerry's, another club. Get out of there about 2:30a.m. If we weren't working till the next evening, we'd then go back to the Buxton, bump into Richard Harris or O'Toole, then up to Covent Garden to the porters' pubs for a last pint and bacon butty, which would take you through till breakfast.' I'm a little hungover just writing that and it's no surprise to learn the company he kept but Gambon wasn't truly one of the renowned Irish hellraisers. He has his own form of 'divilment' (a great Irish word we use for someone who has a bit of a devil in him) and that's his capacity for falsehood.

Gambon is bold as brass, with a twinkle in his eyes and a droll Irish tongue. When he is interviewed, the stories just get madder and more exaggerated all the way through until the weary interviewer asks, 'Have you just made all that up?' 'You'll have to decide for yourself,' he replies. When he comes on the *Late Late Show*, it's possible that half of what he says is made up. Take a look at the James Bond chapter for what could be a prime example of his mischief making.

I like the fact that he tends not to indulge in the preciousness shown by so many in his chosen profession: 'Fundamentally, acting is a deep process of showing off in front of a thousand people, dressing up in costumes and saying, "Look at me." Actors are show-offs, big-headed bastards, egomaniacs. I can't think of any other reason they act. Can you?' In fact, when I went for a drink with him after the *Late Late Show*, he struck me as quite a shy man. He's engaging, gentle and very Irish. I would describe him as mischievously melancholic, with both the mischief and the melancholy being classic Irish traits.

It's a long trek from the streets of suburban Dublin to the hallowed halls of Buckingham Palace but that's where Gambon ended up in 1990 when he was made Commander of the British Empire and he was there for a return visit in 1998 to receive his knighthood. He would henceforth be known as Sir Michael 'please, call me Mike' Gambon.

A biographer of Gambon wrote of him: 'The cliché of English actors – that they are all head and no heart – is belied by Gambon: he projects a rugged masculinity and intensity. In his acting style, he is a bridge between England and the United States.'

That bridge between England and the United States is called Ireland and perhaps it is that which has defined the man as much as any script, any screen or any stage.

SINÉAD CUSACK: a saintly sort

Born 18 February 1948

Acting is a shy person's revenge on the world.

Born in Dublin to actor parents, Sinéad Cusack's first ambition while at convent school was to become a saint. It's something the priests and nuns drum into you so quite a few Irish people go through a phase of coveting canonization, but most of that generation grew out of it relatively quickly – Sinéad certainly did. In her teens she found herself in hot water at school for dramatizing the Profumo affair in front of the headmistress. It wasn't her first acting role, though, as before that, when she was just eleven, her father, legendary actor Cyril Cusack, had cast her as a deaf mute in Kafka's *The Trial*. She joked he probably did it to keep her quiet.

Her mum urged her to study English at University College Dublin but she didn't finish the course, slipping off to work at the Abbey Theatre three months before her finals. She wasn't a saint by any conventional religious standards at this stage and in 1968 found herself accidentally pregnant to a director she was working with. It wasn't an option to have a child out of wedlock in Dublin in the 60s, even if people were doing it across the water in Swinging London. The baby was quietly given up for adoption and Sinéad carried on with her career. Decades later (in 2007), she was re-united with that child (Richard Boyd Barrett), who was by then a socialist member of parliament for a leafy Dublin suburb.

In 1975, she came to London to take over a role in the Boucicault comedy *London Assurance* from Judi Dench. After that she joined the Royal Shakespeare Company and the plaudits began to pour in: two Tony Awards for *Much Ado about Nothing* (1985) and *Rock 'n' Roll* (2008), the 1998 *Evening Standard* Best Actress Award and Critics' Circle Theatre Award for her role in *Our Lady of Sligo* (1998). And in 2013, her old alma mater Trinity College finally gave her an honorary degree and doctorate of letters, forty-five years after she was a student there.

Meanwhile, she became thespian royalty when in 1978 she married English actor Jeremy Irons. Their marriage has been one of the longest in luvviedom (over thirty years now) and the acting gene has travelled through three generations: Sinead's parents, her sisters Niamh and Sorcha, her half-sister Catherine, and her son Max Irons.

She's a very Irish actress despite living in London for almost forty years, being married to a quintessentially English actor and most famous for her roles in England's own Shakespearean canon. She can do any accent a script requires but still speaks with a beautiful, soft Irish accent and seems to have an Irish sensibility. There must be pressure when you are part of a classic acting dynasty like the Cusacks, but she carries it lightly, and always with dignity.

FIONA SHAW: the thespian's thespian

Born 10 July 1958

> I live among the English and have always found them to be very honest in their business dealings. They are noble, hard-working and anxious to do the right thing. But joy eludes them, they lack the joy that the Irish have.

She may be best known for playing Harry Potter's aunt (see Chapter 10) but Fiona Shaw is probably the greatest theatre actress of her generation – in Britain, Ireland or the United States. She's won awards galore – the *Evening Standard* Theatre Award for her Medea, the Drama Desk Award for Outstanding One-Person Show for *The Waste Land*, an honorary CBE from Her Majesty, the medal of Officier des Arts et des Lettres from France – and she's even got her portrait up in London's National Portrait Gallery. But at heart she's an Irish woman, with a distinctly Celtic take on the world.

Fiona Wilson was born in Cork to an eye surgeon father and physicist mother. She studied philosophy at University College Cork, then came over to RADA in London for classical acting training at the place which is notoriously difficult to get into but has turned out more renowned actors than any other. She graduated in the same period as a whole slew of other talent, including Jonathan Pryce, Juliet Stevenson, Alan Rickman and Belfast boy Kenneth Branagh, then walked straight into a National Theatre production of Sheridan's *The Rivals*. Other theatre followed: *Electra*, *Machinal*, *Medea* and *Hedda Gabler*, to name but a few. Soon, whenever a strong dramatic female lead came along, Fiona Shaw was the name at the top of the wish list.

In 1995, she began to work with director Deborah Warner and theirs became one of the most exciting creative partnerships in modern theatre. Warner cast Shaw as the male lead in *Richard II*, then helped her to develop her one-woman production of *The Waste Land*, which toured extensively, including a stint in Dublin, in a venue that Shaw describes as 'an abandoned English fort on top of a hill in Phoenix Park, in one of the low-dome-ceilinged 18th-century bunkers where the colonists kept their gunpowder.' They've done Euripides, Brecht, Ibsen, Shakespeare and Sophocles, each play going through long, punishing rehearsal periods until both are satisfied that it is just right. Shaw is a lapsed Catholic with strong views on Catholicism: '[It] awakens philosophical questions in bright children by trying to strangle those questions before birth.' Some hypothesize that the collaboration between her and Warner works so well because of the contrast between Warner's stoic, calm Quaker beliefs and Shaw's fiery lapsed Catholicism. Whatever the chemistry was, they pushed forwards the boundaries for women in theatre and for theatre itself.

Shaw has made films as well, playing Daniel Day Lewis's doctor in *My Left Foot* (1989), Mrs Nugent in *The Butcher Boy* (1997, based on the Patrick McCabe novel) and, more recently, the palm-reading witch in *True Blood*, as well as her classic turn as Harry Potter's Muggle aunt.

Shaw lives in London now but often visits her family in Ireland, where she says she likes the attitude to life: 'There once was a demographic survey done to determine if money was connected to happiness and Ireland was the only place where this did not turn out to be true.' Maybe it's because the Irish got used to living without it for so many centuries that they learned to have a laugh without dipping into their pockets. All they needed to do was hang out with characters like my next thespian, and life would be a laugh a minute.

CHRIS O'DOWD: class clown

Born 9 October 1979

We all want to be Daniel Day Lewis but in the end, I'm Jerry Lewis.

One of the newest additions to the 'Irish success abroad' story is cheeky master of gormless but beguiling comedy acting Chris O'Dowd. Goofy, bold and a little bit loud, Chris belongs to the unapologetic generation of Irish who joined the multi-cultural London landscape in a post-peace-process world, unburdened by politics and abhorrent headlines, and unshackled by random racism. This has meant that his Irishness simply doesn't feature. I suspect there are very few offices in Britain that don't have at least one Irish person working in them nowadays, so it didn't raise any eyebrows that he became a sitcom star playing an Irish guy in an office in the smash hit *The IT Crowd*.

154

Born into an 'arty' family (Dad was a graphic designer who played guitar in pubs in Boyle, Mum was a psychotherapist), Chris has admitted to being an attention-seeker as a child. As the youngest of five, he may have felt the need to shout loudest or jump highest in order to gain the ear of his betters. Towering above his classmates, Chris was six feet tall by his eleventh birthday and when girls entered the fray, it was Chris as Lewis rather than Day Lewis who showed up: 'I was the guy who girls found funny and they'd ask me what my male friends thought of them.'

When it came to his future, Chris had a choice: he could stay in Boyle and work at a credit card company or the fish factory – or he could go to college in Dublin and investigate life beyond County Roscommon. Unlike many of the other subjects in this book, Chris never hated his hometown; in fact, it defines him in many respects. He took to the Gaelic football fields where he was handy enough to play on the Roscommon minor team, although sport was never really a vocation or an ambition. Described as a 'bright' student by a schoolteacher, he studied for an arts degree at University College Dublin, where he aspired to be a speechwriter but instead found an outlet for his burgeoning personality through drama. He explains: 'I don't know whether it was the narcissism or the attention-seeking, or the opportunity to explore characteristics I don't have as much as the characters I was playing have. And also I like hanging out with actors: the guys are generally fun, the girls are generally loose.'

With all that hanging out and all those loose girls, it is probably no surprise that Chris left University College Dublin without completing his degree. He headed for the London Academy of Music and Dramatic Art, an expensive course for aspiring thespians, but (like Graham Norton) didn't complete this either.

While he tried to break into the acting world, bills were paid courtesy of a job answering phones at a call centre, which is London's version of waiting tables or pumping gas in LA. He then did some ads for Pizza Hut and got bit parts in heavy films like *Conspiracy of Silence* (2003) and *Vera Drake* (2004). In Ireland he played the part of a 'dork' in medical drama *The Clinic* (2003–5) so convincingly that his sisters suggested no acting was required.

In 2005, a big part in a small movie saw Chris win a Scottish BAFTA for his role as a jaded Irish comedian in *Festival*, his first-ever award. It was around this time that *Father Ted* co-creator Graham Linehan (see Chapter 2) was looking for someone to play Roy, a character in a sitcom he was writing about an IT department. He wasn't specifically looking to cast an Irish actor but Chris wandered into an audition 'and just blew us away. I just couldn't say no to him'. In the series, Roy has a distinctly Irish accent that Chris was more than happy to retain. As he explains: 'There are so many Irish people in London that it's nice we barely mention the fact that he's Irish. There's a thing that Stephen Rea said, that there's no reason for me to change my accent unless there's a reason. And I like that. I'm very conscious of that voice needing to be heard.'

The series was a hit and the parts began rolling in for Roscommon's favourite son. A small but not insignificant role in the Jack Black vehicle *Gulliver's Travels* in 2010 was followed by a more prominent part in the box-office comedy hit of 2011, *Bridesmaids*, where he played the part of a cop called Rhodes. Unassuming, sweet, awkward, a bit shy and useless with women and yet attractive at the same time, it was a part Chris was born to play. And for anyone from Ireland watching this all-American film featuring a cop with an unapologetic Irish brogue, it was a moment of some pride! (Spoiler alert: he even gets the girl in the end.) As far as

156

Chris is concerned, the accent is part of the charm: 'They say that the power of a word comes from the consonants and the feeling comes from the vowels. Because we elongate our vowels so much, there's much more feeeelings in our woooords . . . I'm not the first Irishman to do that. Every barkeeper in New York knows about it.'

More recently, Chris returned home to his beloved Roscommon where he filmed the comedy series *Moone Boy*, based on his own upbringing. It's a credit to his standing among his peers that the cast is of the highest comedy calibre with Steve Coogan and Johnny Vegas among those seen around the streets of Chris's hometown. It's also rather impressive that he managed to convince Sky 1 that a surreal comedy based entirely in a small Irish town would make for good television. To the question of whether or not the show will get lost in translation, Chris is stoical: 'If the audience outside Ireland doesn't understand what they're saying, I don't care. People in England watch *The Wire* and get it, so we're not putting any subtitles on this. It's a very loving look at where I grew up.' The gamble paid off and a second series was commissioned.

And for the record, the guy got the girl in real life when Chris got engaged to TV presenter girlfriend Dawn Porter at an infamous suicide spot near where she was brought up. He announced the joyous news on Twitter: 'So bored of all this happiness and sex I'm getting married.' They now live with their Jack Russell, name of Potato.

I've had Chris on the *Late Late Show* and found him a happy-go-lucky guy. We went for a few drinks afterwards (I feel a theme coming on . . .) and he was very good fun, good company. He's riding on the crest of a wave at the moment and I wouldn't write him off as 'only' a comedy actor. As he hurtles towards forty, he continues to play the part of put-upon good guy with a big heart, a sloppy demeanour and an inclination to play it for laughs. Watch this space.

*   *   *

There are lots of actors missing from this list but most of them, while having a profile in the UK, don't live there and so aren't included. You'll find more actors in the Hellraisers, Harry Potter and Bond chapters but honourable mentions should be made here for a few. Brenda Fricker played nurse Megan Roach on British screens every Saturday night in sixty-five episodes of *Casualty* and won an Oscar for her role in *My Left Foot*, but although she has spent a lot of time in the UK she remains part and parcel of Dublin life. Cillian Murphy was born in Cork and lives in London but has made his name doing big Hollywood movies like *Batman Begins*, *The Dark Knight* and *Inception*, so he's not particularly associated with the British acting scene. Colm Meaney has worked a lot in the UK but has made his home in Ireland and Spain, so he's not in. Comedian Pat Shortt (described by the *Irish Times* as a 'national treasure') was widely praised for his performance in London's West End in *The Cripple of Inishmaan* opposite Daniel Radcliffe in summer 2013, but he's one proud Limerick man and hasn't lowered the anchor in London just yet. It's not an exact science but I stick by my criteria and will do so as well in the next chapter, about musicians.

We all love our music in Ireland. I'm not saying we all have exceptional musical talent – that would be an exaggeration too far – but the people I'm going to cover next have brought their own distinct brand of Irishness to British concert venues and TV screens, and the book wouldn't be complete without them.

8

THE
MUSICIANS

ON A GOOD NIGHT OUT IN IRELAND, at around one or two in the morning when conversation has been exhausted, fights started and resolved, relationships begun and ended, and the lower-hanging fruits have headed to bed, someone at the end of the table or in the corner of the room will start to sing. It might be 'The Rocky Road to Dublin' or it could be 'I Wanna Marry You'; it doesn't matter as long as we can all mumble through the chorus with gusto while the competent singer gets on with the business of remembering the words. This, my friends, is what we call the 'comeallye' – as in 'come in all of you and sing along'. There are no screens with words to help, there is no band playing too loudly, it's just a musical footnote to what was probably a fine night out. It might not be the exclusive preserve of the Irish but I like to think that we do it better than anyone else because we are musical as a nation, can hold a tune for the most part and much of our history gets turned into a song almost as soon as the event is over.

Take the Clancy Brothers and Tommy Makem, for example, holding court at Madison Square Garden in the 1960s, sweat pouring off them as they belted their way through the finest folk tunes Ireland had to offer. On paper, they were the most unlikely bunch but they were charismatic and engrossing to watch. They sang for President John F. Kennedy at one point, such was their popularity. Always clad in flat caps and big white woolly Aran sweaters (which probably accounted for the sweat), their repertoire included drinking songs like 'Come Fill Your Glass with Us' and freedom songs like 'The Irish Uprising' and 'Bold Fenian Sons' alongside traditional numbers like 'Marie's Wedding' and 'Will Ye Go, Lassie, Go'. They were great story-tellers, and great fun: hard-drinking, hard-living boys who sang and played guitar as if their lives depended on it. Later in his life I had the good fortune to interview Liam Clancy a few times before his death in 2009, and he had a fierce twinkle in his eye so that I always felt there was bold-ness around the corner. I recall watching him rehearse 'Those Were the Days' when he was coming on *Tubridy Tonight*, a chat show I was presenting at the time, and he sang each time as if it was his first. It was inspiring to watch someone in his seventies being so professional and dedicated to the music.

Besides singing, the other best-known type of traditional Irish music is fiddle-playing. The fiddle is one of our national instru-ments. In the early twentieth century two Michaels, Coleman and Gorman, both from County Sligo, did a lot to popularize fiddle-playing with their live concerts and albums, while John Doherty, a traveller from County Donegal, became the man to invite to your house party, where he'd borrow someone else's fiddle and strike up a tune. There are different styles of playing the fiddle in the differ-ent regions, and it can be a fiercely competitive subject so I'll move on quickly before I say anything contentious and start a row.

Both the Clancy Brothers and the fiddlers helped to popularize traditional Irish styles of music and can be seen as precursors of modern Irish bands like Clannad, the Corrs and the Chieftains.

Other Irish musicians of the second half of the twentieth century were a bit slow off the mark when it came to rock and pop music. We still had show bands and ballrooms of romance while the Beatles and the Stones were kickstarting a cultural and sexual revolution across the water.

Ireland caught up some time in the 70s and we started producing our own take on the current trends – and a lot of our musicians became extraordinarily successful. Given that we're only a tiny country, we punch well above our weight when it comes to musicians. U2 have sold over 150 million albums worldwide and *Rolling Stone* magazine ranks them as number twenty-two in its list of the 100 Greatest Artists of All Time. Rory Gallagher sold more than 30 million albums with his own brand of blues-rock and still has a huge following in Ireland. Phil Lynott formed the massively successful band Thin Lizzy and had hits with 'The Boys Are Back in Town' and the very Irish 'Whisky in the Jar', among others. Sinéad O'Connor's version of 'Nothing Compares 2 U', delivered in her unique, haunting voice, made number one in dozens of countries around the planet. And Enya – well, after leaving Clannad she became one of the world's best-selling solo artists of all time with her unique brand of Celtic folk melodies over a synthesizer backing track. It's a mixed bag but that's part of the success of Irish music and its propensity to travel: there's a little something for all tastes.

In this chapter, as in the rest of the book, I'm going to chat about my own eclectic selection of the ones who came to Britain and had a particular impact on British culture – starting with the rocking granddaddy of them all.

VAL DOONICAN: the singing Seanchaí

Born 3 February 1927

There's still a hard core who believe that I am Eamonn
Andrews and Val Doonican's love child.

– Terry Wogan

Val Doonican is from Waterford in Ireland's Sunny South East
and, like Eamonn and Terry, became one of the most influential
ambassadors for Ireland in the UK during the Troubles. I interviewed him back around 2001, when he was still touring, and
found him very genial, kind, elegant and old-school – exactly what
you'd expect from the man who sat crooning in a rocking chair on
the BBC every Saturday night in his *Val Doonican Show*. There's
always been something homely about him, with his toothy grin,
cuddly jumper and warm personality, and his show was certainly a
very unthreatening hour of television back in the day.

Val was the youngest of eight children and the family weren't
well-off but he always speaks of having a happy childhood, in
particular enjoying time foraging in the countryside with his
father until his early death when Val was fourteen. His hobby was
writing music or harmonizing songs with his friends, and his first
public appearance was at a Waterford fête where he memorably
sang 'We're Three Caballeros' with a friend. They began touring
Ireland in a caravan, singing for their supper, and got their first
break when they were given a job singing a jingle for a sausage
commercial to the tune of the 'Mexican Hat Dance'. Then in 1951,
Val was approached by a band called the Four Ramblers, and that
brought him across the Irish Sea to a brand-new British career.

He rambled around Britain – getting married along the way – and in 1963 his solo career was launched on *Sunday Night at the London Palladium* (like that of his compatriot Dave Allen). As Val quips, 'I was an overnight success after seventeen years.' He initially became known for his comic Irish songs, such as 'O'Rafferty's Motor Car' and 'Paddy McGinty's Goat', but had his first chart hit with 'Walk Tall' in 1964 and after that the hits just kept rolling in.

The title of his 1968 album *Val Doonican Rocks, But Gently* sums up the man. You weren't going to be deafened at a Val Doonican gig. He didn't throw himself off the stage or rip off his V-neck while eating a bat. He's more like an Irish Bing Crosby or Perry Como, who brought the UK a very non-threatening brand of Irishness at a time when the headlines were dominated by reports of terrorist atrocities but Val kept on rocking. Gently.

GILBERT O'SULLIVAN: moody bluesman
Born 1 December 1946

I write pop songs. End of story. That's all I wanted to do. That's all I want to do. And that's all I continue to want to do.

Reeling in the Years is a programme that tells the story of modern Ireland, showing the history, politics and pop culture of a given year through archive footage, music and smart subtitles. It's repeated on RTÉ all the time and still scores in the weekly top ten most-watched programmes. For a lot of younger Irish people, this is how they learn about some of the biggest events and best music of the twentieth century. And that's how I came across Gilbert O'Sullivan, in a clip showing a young man at his piano in front of a massive crowd of adoring fans (are there any other kind?). The man has hair. Lots of hair. And he is at the top of his game. His name is Gilbert O'Sullivan and he hails from Waterford, the county that previously gave us Val Doonican.

The popstar with the big 'G' on his sweater is defined by that shaggy haircut and the infectious melodies that made him as big a star as Elton John back in the early 70s. But what happened to the boy from Waterford? Where's he been hiding since then? I've interviewed him a couple of times since his heyday because he comes over to Ireland quite a bit but he doesn't seem to me to identify himself as Irish in quite the same way as most other characters in this book.

Perhaps it's because the O'Sullivan family left Waterford when young Raymond Edward O'Sullivan (Gilbert's real name) was just thirteen. They went to live in Swindon, Wiltshire, where his father hoped to make it in the building trade, but sadly he died two years after their arrival. Gilbert started writing his own songs and played drums in a band founded by Rick Davies, who would later find fame in Supertramp. He got himself a recording contract with CBS in 1967 but the hits weren't coming until Gordon Mills of MAM Records took him on and restyled him, among other things giving him the name Gilbert in a fun take on the songwriting duo Gilbert *and* Sullivan.

The first hit, 'Nothing Rhymed', came in 1970, followed by his most famous songs 'Alone Again (Naturally)' (1972, about a guy who is suicidal after his fiancée jilts him at the altar), 'Clair' (1972, about Gordon Mills's young daughter) and 'Get Down' (1973, a command to a dog!). There were seven Top Ten hits in the UK, and four Top Ten albums over a five-year period, and Gilbert O'Sullivan songs blared from every radio in the UK, the United

States and Japan. A falling-out with Gordon Mills led to a five-year court case, which O'Sullivan won in 1982, but it meant a hiatus in his recording career. There was another court case in 1991 when he sued rapper Biz Markie for sampling 'Alone Again (Naturally)', and he won when the judge compared sampling to theft. But somehow he never got back to the position of chart domination he had enjoyed, although he kept writing and singing and playing.

In 2001, he brought out an album entitled *Irlish* about the generation who, like him, were Irish by birth but came to England for a better life. He toured Ireland and went on the *Late Late Show* to promote it, and Irish viewers strained to hear the hint of an Irish brogue in his speaking voice. 'I'm one of you,' he claimed, despite living in Guernsey with his family. He writes songs that you find yourself humming in the shower, and he has a poetic way with lyrics, but not many of them hark back to his Irish roots.

By contrast to the jumpers and pet dogs and easy-listening ballads, my next subject is an Irish success story cut from a different kind of cloth entirely.

BOB GELDOF: Celtic motormouth
Born 5 October 1951

> Did God knock on the wrong door by mistake and when it was opened by this scruffy Irishman, think, Oh, what the hell, he'll do?
>
> *– Life Magazine*

I've met Bob several times and he's a tricky old interviewee, like a bucking bronco you have to stay on for fifteen minutes without coming a cropper. He could come out with anything at all: 'This interview's shite' or 'I'm off now.' And he's a campaigner so if you've got fifteen minutes of TV, he's got one issue and you have twenty questions prepared, you may find it impossible to stop him gabbing on for thirteen of those minutes about his issue alone. The *Late Late Show* is live, so I can't edit it into shape later. That's why I have a slight feeling of dread when I know Bob's coming on – but, having said that, the last time he was great and there were no problems at all.

Belying his appearance, behaviour and the causes he went on to espouse, Bob Geldof was born into a very comfortable, middle-class existence in the affluent Dublin suburb of Blackrock. He went to a posh school and, on the face of it, had a charmed childhood. The charm was swiftly and cruelly removed when Bob's mother, Eve, died from a brain haemorrhage aged just forty-four. Angry and confused, Bob became a rebel at the Catholic all-boys' school he attended. Asthma excused him from playing any sport but his sisters' love of music was passed on to him so that when it came to casting for the school musicals, Bob (whose repertoire included most of Cliff Richard's back catalogue) was happy to accept a role.

At home, young Bob had a tempestuous relationship with his father, and an Irish temper that saw him rail against authority figures and perceived injustices in general. Academic pursuits were shelved in favour of pastimes and hobbies. Hanging around his local record store was one such habit and it was here Bob listened to the Beatles, the Who and the Stones: 'Jagger fascinated me. Suddenly my big mouth was acceptable. Suddenly my scruffiness was something to be emulated rather than sneered at. The Rolling Stones looked and sounded like they were saying "f**k you" to everything. They were my boys.'

A reader of Camus, Sartre and Kafka, this 'smart messer with a heart' joined the Simon Community, a charity that helped the homeless on the streets of Dublin, and we can see a pattern starting to form. After school, Bob headed to England for a summer where, among other things, he followed the route of many other Irish immigrants into the building trade and helped build the M25: 'It was a nice way to spend the summer with a book, listening to Slade on Radio 1 and watching the cars go by.'

Following a stint working for a local paper in Canada, Bob came home and became front man for Mark Skid and the Y-Fronts, a name that changed to Night Life Thugs and then, after a passage Bob saw in Woody Guthrie's autobiography *Bound for Glory*, became the Boomtown Rats.

The Rats grew big enough for them to enter the punk cauldron bubbling in the UK at the time. The Pistols and the Damned were among the many bands of the era competing to make the most noise and cause the most controversy. This was a milieu tailor-made for Bob Geldof. Success duly followed and the late 70s were his playground. Top Ten singles like 'Rat Trap', 'Banana Republic' and 'I Don't Like Mondays' made him a star and he loved it. The songs are full of political anger, though. He was constantly angry at someone for something.

By the mid-1980s, Bob's musical career was on the wane but his passion was unaffected. Watching Michael Buerk reporting on the Ethiopian famine, he was struck by the pictures he was looking at, describing them as 'people who were so shrunken by starvation that they looked like beings from another planet'. By now a father, he went to bed that night and barely slept a wink. It was a simple yet profound moment that would yield arguably the biggest international push ever for charity. Using his ability to cajole, convince and coerce, Bob gathered together as many peers as he could to record 'Do They Know Its Christmas?'. This was swiftly followed by a mammoth push to organize Live Aid, an extraordinary global jukebox on 13 July 1985 that linked gigs in London's Wembley Stadium and the JFK Stadium in Philadelphia. Some 1.9 billion viewers in 150 countries around the world tuned in to witness this unprecedented moment of history. Over $140 million was raised in an era before Facebook, YouTube, Twitter and the rest.

I remember watching Live Aid. I was twelve and viewing it at home but my older brother was actually at the event so there was great excitement at our place. From Bob cursing on live television to Queen's show-stealing appearance and on to that terrible footage of starving children wandering about gaunt and helpless to the soundtrack of the Cars, the events of the day have stayed with me. Maybe the feeling was intensified for us because it was an Irishman running the show. At that moment in time, it was as if Bob was the only story in town. He became a global phenomenon with his ceaseless drive to help Africa get off its knees.

Although his own life became what he called 'part of the national soap opera' following his wife Paula Yates's departure from their marriage and her tragic death thereafter, Bob kept focused on the two things that appeared to matter most to him: family and world poverty. The former he kept as private as possible, the latter he shouted about from every available hilltop. Attempting to emulate the success of Live Aid, he pulled together Live 8 in 2005 with a message to 'Make Poverty History'. A lofty if vague notion, the event was still considered a success. He now channels that famous anger into his campaigns for whatever is on his mind at the time: fathers' rights, AIDS, world peace . . . It seems to me that if there was a hole in the bag he was doing his shopping with, he'd campaign against bags with holes in them. He's just one of life's campaigners.

One of his many legacies in Britain is that most British people now think we Irish all talk like Bob Geldof. When I hear a British person trying an Irish accent, it's normally a bad Geldof: 'I loick you'. When Alan Partridge gave it a try, he sounded Yorkshire. Of course, to capture the real Bob Geldof you need to pepper your speech with profanities . . . Despite (or perhaps because of) the bad language he has become an enormously influential (and wealthy) businessman through his TV production companies Planet 24, Ten Alps and Pretend. I could have put him in Chapter 12, the business chapter, but it's for his music, and Live Aid in particular, that we know and love him best.

In September 2013, I interviewed Geldof on the *Late Late Show*. He was on to perform 'Looking After Number One' with his newly reformed Boomtown Rats. During rehearsals, we got into a long conversation about how his angry songs of yesteryear have become relevant once more with the difficult position in which Ireland currently found itself. Just three days later, I phoned him on my radio show after it was announced Bob was going to be the first Irishman in space. I thought it was a joke, but the man himself confirmed the story and promised he would take an Irish flag with him. Gregarious, curmudgeonly and compelling, Bob Geldof hasn't changed and now he's off to hang out with the proper stars. As one headline put it, 'We have Geld-off . . .'.

It's been a remarkable life thus far for Bob Geldof. He has travelled a long way from the classrooms that bored him in Blackrock and from the bedsits that housed him in London. He's been knighted by the Queen, although he's not officially allowed to use the 'Sir' prefix because he's not one of her subjects. He was made a Freeman of Dublin by the Irish people, an honour that gives him the right to graze his sheep on Dublin's St Stephen's Green. I don't think Bob has sheep, but if he did . . .

He has medals, doctorates and awards coming out of his ears and yet, having met and interviewed him many times, I reckon that he hasn't changed. Shabby, craggy and meticulously unkempt, there isn't much to separate the angry schoolboy and the latter-day saint.

THE NOLAN SISTERS: aka the naughty Nolans

Anne (born 1950), Denise (born 1952),
Maureen (born 1954), Linda (born 1959),
Bernie (1960–2013), Coleen (born 1965)

I'm in the mood for dancing, romancin',
Ooh, I'm givin' it all tonight.

In the late 70s, when Bob was letting off steam with 'Rat Trap' and 'I Don't Like Mondays', he was sharing the charts with a girl band that had quite a different style. The Rats and the Nolans were polar opposites, if truth be told. Perhaps the only thing Bob and the Nolan sisters had in common was being born in Dublin and being musicians. That, and the fact that they have been entertaining interviewees on my chat shows . . .

In 2009, Maureen, Linda, Bernie and Coleen came on the *Late Late Show* to publicize their comeback tour. They're lively women and there were four of them so it was amusingly unruly. Who do you talk to when you're interviewing four famous sisters? I reckon it's like a fish tank. You put some food on the top and whoever gets there first wins; that's who's going to be running the show. In this case, it was the late great Bernie, who died a month ago at the time of writing. She was the sparkiest and although I addressed questions to everyone round the group, it was Bernie who came in with the great one-liners and to whom the others turned, semi-acknowledging her leadership.

Tommy and Maureen Nolan, the girls' parents, had worked as singers around Ireland and the first five girls were born in the Dublin area, where they have fond memories of going to the seaside in Bray. In 1962, they decamped to Blackpool and a family group, the Singing Nolans, was launched. In 1974, Mum and Dad decided to stay in the wings and let the girls sing on their own as the Nolan Sisters and then the Nolans. There was lots of hard graft and slogging away as the support act for other bands until their big hit 'I'm in the Mood for Dancing' came out at the end of 1979 and rocketed up to number three in the UK charts. It was exactly the right time for a cheesy upbeat disco hit that you could jiggle along to no matter what your proficiency as a dancer. The Nolans were especially big in Japan, for some reason, winning the grand prize at the 1981 Tokyo Music Festival, and then recording English-language cover versions of a number of Japanese hits. They carried on through the 80s and 90s before hanging up their Spandex in favour of other career paths.

Bernie became an actress and starred in *Brookside* and *The Bill* on British television. Coleen became one of the contestants in *Dancing on Ice* (or, as she calls it, *Falling on Ice*) and a regular panellist on *Loose Women*. And the girls worked in musicals and shows, such as *Blood Brothers*.

There were famous fallings-out. Denise left the group early on to pursue a solo career, and both she and Anne got cross that they were not included in the 2009 comeback tour, but all came together when the news broke that Bernie had terminal cancer. She thought she'd beaten it in 2011, but found a lump in 2012 and the doctors had to give her the hard news that it had spread to her brain, lungs, liver and bones.

It's appropriate and heartening to know that the Nolans made their peace in the end. Being together as a family at Christmas can be a trial for some, so try touring Europe together! I suspect that the Nolans' greatest contribution to the Anglo-Irish story will be 'I'm in the mood', that utterly addictive ear worm that drags even the least able dancers among us to the floor at the wedding we don't even want to be at . . .

And talking of dancing . . .

RIVERDANCE: a reinvented art form

Born 30 April 1994

The problem with being Irish . . . is having Riverdance
on your back. It's a burden at times.

– Roddy Doyle

So, there we all were in 1994, watching the *Eurovision Song Contest* being held in Dublin. Some were cheering, many jeering, but all watching. It got to the interval act and just as the nation started to head for the kitchen to make tea, a celestial voice rang out, which was joined by a ghostly choir and then a drum beat. The tea was forgotten as we walked backwards into the sitting room to see what this was. Before we knew it there were these dancers who appeared to be Irish dancing – but they couldn't be? Where were the curly wigs and Celtic crosses? Where was the fake tan and what happened to the clunky black shoes that were better suited to a convent? These dancers had long legs and bouncing tresses (the girls!), while the men were buffed and easy for the ladies to look at. As a nation, we were confused, mesmerized, gob-smacked but excited. Was this where we were as a country? Vibrant, pulsating, confident . . . sexy?

The music reached a crescendo, the drums had us in a frenzy, the lead dancers were looking sideways at each other, smiling as if to say 'Jesus, this is great' and at last, the final high-octane beats exploded and with them the auditorium, and with them families leaped from their couches around the country. Something happened, something had changed, a corner had been turned.

In the junior infants at school, we were taught Irish dancing for about five minutes. I've repressed the memory but I'm sure it was nothing like this. Purists tell me the Irish dancing in Riverdance is not the 'real thing' but as far as I can see it's breathed new life into an old art. If you want culture to travel and stay alive, you have to be prepared to change your hemlines with the times.

After that *Eurovision* premiere, the Riverdance stage show was introduced by Terry Wogan at the 1994 Royal Variety Show and the Riverdance single dominated the charts all summer. The troupe began to tour, from Dublin to London and New York, and everywhere they went tickets were selling out. And it hasn't ended. Twenty years later, they are still instantly recognizable as a symbol of traditional Irish music and dance, and have been spoofed by enough comedians to give them icon status. (In *Family Guy, Buffy the Vampire Slayer* and by Stavros Flatley in *Britain's Got Talent*, to name but a few.)

The lead dancers at that *Eurovision* premiere were Irish dancing champions Jean Butler and Michael Flatley. Both are second-generation Irish Americans, whose parents had pushed them to strive and succeed. Flatley says he was dragged to Irish dance classes by his ears, but stuck around because 'there were lots of pretty girls'. He stayed with the Riverdance show for just a year after their auspicious debut then left 'due to differences over creative control'. He then formed his own shows – *Lord of the Dance*, *Feet of Flames* and *Celtic Tiger* – and danced his way into the record books. Notably, in 1989 he had set a Guinness World Record for tap-dancing at a speed of twenty-eight taps per second. I'm exhausted just writing that! He also got the record in 1999 and 2000 for being the world's highest-paid dancer, earning $1.6 million per week. And his legs became the world's most expensive when he insured them for $40 million. That's a lot of world records.

There are those who knock Riverdance for being a little hokey, but twenty years ago, it was considered a very modern phenomenon. And given its enduring popularity around the world, I doubt the show's creators are too concerned about the naysayers.

*   *   *

So there you have it: from 60s crooner to angry punk, from commercial popsters to manic dancers. Again I'm missing loads. I could have included Siobhan Fahey of hugely successful girl group Bananarama and then the acclaimed Shakespears Sister, but despite the very Irish name she only lived in Dublin until the age of two. Maybe I should have included Rory Gallagher, who was born and raised in County Donegal. He moved to London in the 70s when his musical career took off but always made a point of touring in Ireland at least once a year, at a time when other musicians were staying away because of the political unrest.

You may have blanked this one from your memory, but in 1968 the esteemed Richard Harris launched a pop career and had an international hit with Jimmy Webb's bizarrely brilliant 'MacArthur Park', in which an emotional Harris bemoans the fact that 'someone left the cake out in the rain' and continues in that vein for some seven minutes. Enjoying life in the music world, Harris kept on going, releasing many albums and touring with the Phil Coulter orchestra in 1972. But let's just say that U2 never had any fear that he would wrest their crown from them.

Depending on their musical taste, the British may not thank the Irish for all (or any) of these performers. It's probably true to say that Ireland kept the best musicians back at home. But Sir Bob is a towering giant when it comes to influence in the world of music, as Live Aid has spawned dozens of imitators, all raising money for charity and helping the needy of the planet.

Before we leave musicians, there's one more phenomenon I should mention that has a distinct Irish link. You may not like the music but millions of screaming girls would tell you you've had your fun and it's our turn now! Cynics may want to skip ahead a few pages as we briefly discuss the Irish contribution to the much-debated world of . . . boy bands.

9

THE
BOY BANDS

In the twenty-first century, there's an insatiable appetite to get famous fast by any means possible. Once upon a time, fame was achieved by hard graft. U2 sweated it out through years of small-town gigs in church halls and demos recorded on home equipment after the band formed in 1976. Their first properly successful album, *War*, didn't come out till 1983 and it was their performance at Live Aid in 1985 that really cemented their position as global superstars. Nowadays, kids want success overnight, without the graft, and one way they can go about it is by striking it lucky on the right TV show.

Whether you want them or not, Ireland has made a major contribution to the boy band culture and has exported several band members over the water to the UK – as well as one of the most influential boy band svengalis. Young girls go crazy for Irish boy band exports, screaming every bit as hard as their grannies used to do for the Beatles. Merchandise floods out of the warehouses, stadium gigs are sold out, and parents' credit cards creak and groan, so I can't see the phenomenon going away any time soon.

It's interesting to look at the lives of the individual band members. I've interviewed quite a few of them on the *Late Late Show* and the phrase 'Be careful what you wish for' often comes to mind. Fame and fortune didn't come cheap for some, with bankruptcies, substance abuse issues and toxic relationships all reported in glaring detail in the media. This kind of attention is part and parcel of modern celebrity and, as you would expect, some of them have dealt with it better than others.

This chapter is not a morality tale, though. It's a look at how Irish boy bands have come over and had an impact in the UK, so we have to start by meeting the man who brought the open boy band audition to Irish soil.

LOUIS WALSH: the street-smart Svengali

Born 5 August 1952

> Deep down I am nice . . . but sometimes I portray something else. If I was watching me on TV I would probably think: 'He's a little bollix. Who does he think he is?'

Louis Walsh means one thing to a certain generation and something completely different to the next, so your view of him depends on your age. He came on to the radar for me in 1999 when RTÉ started showing *Reeling in the Years*. Every so often this impish face with a head of curly hair would pop up in the background at some *Eurovision* contest or other, and I thought, 'Wonder what he's got to do with anything?'

I first heard the word 'Svengali' at school in relation to Rasputin, the scheming Russian monk, and the next time I heard it was in relation to Mr Louis Walsh and his association with the boy bands he managed. Then there was his whole Simon Cowell period.

So, *Eurovision*, boy bands and then *X Factor* – that covers three generations and, knowing Louis the bit that I do, there's plenty more to come.

I've met and interviewed him dozens of times in Irish TV and radio studios. He's a regular fixture on any show I do, and is a great interviewee because he's always full of anecdotes. He tends not to have a filter, which is great, but he's wily enough not to get himself into any trouble (unless it's planned for maximum media coverage, of course). He loves a bit of juice, like a human version of *Heat* magazine, and is a great businessman as well with a sharp commercial eye for a band.

As a young boy growing up in Kiltimagh, County Mayo, Louis was never one for Gaelic football or hurling and he wasn't going to end up on a bar stool at the local, watching television and playing darts. While the lads in his class followed the ups and downs of the local and county teams, young Louis could be found at the newsagent, patiently awaiting the latest edition of *NME*, which was specially ordered for him from Dublin. If he wasn't squirrelled away in his bedroom reading his favourite paper, he was most likely listening to the tracks being played on Radio Luxembourg. Essentially it was always about music for him.

He was the second oldest of nine brothers and sisters, and Louis' mum Maureen had hopes that he might enter the priesthood. A brief stint as an altar boy was quite enough of a religious experience for her son, who had other plans in mind. By the time he was thirteen, Louis and his sister Evelyn eagerly anticipated Saturdays when they hopped on the bus to Castlebar to buy the latest records. As he got older, Louis made his way to the local ballrooms to watch his favourite showbands of the day. Never a fan of academic pursuits, Louis headed for Dublin as soon as he hit seventeen and found a job as a dogsbody for a music agent. It was the perfect training ground for a would-be music mogul as the dog-eat-dog world of the Irish showband business taught the Mayo man a thing or two: 'If you could work with ballroom promoters in Ireland you could work with anybody. Some would send the bands home without money. The showbands were great. The promoters were just dreadful to deal with.'

Louis' life-changing moment took place on a local bus in his home county of Mayo. It was 1975 and he found himself sitting beside a singer called Johnny Logan. Louis became Johnny's manager and within five years Logan had won the *Eurovision Song Contest* with 'What's Another Year', which went on to become a number one hit in ten countries. Even after that, he complains, not many people came to Logan's concerts and his other records didn't sell in the huge numbers they deserved, even after he won the *Eurovision* again in 1987 and wrote the winning song in 1992.

Learning how to sell pop music to the Irish was a good training ground for Louis, and in the 1990s he achieved national and then international fame courtesy of a series of clever moves and intelligent investments.

Watching enviously as Take That stormed the charts across the water in the early 1990s, Louis hatched a plan to assemble a similar act in Ireland. Using the tried and tested route of a newspaper ad, Louis put out a call in 1993 for those interested in being part of a band. Following a series of auditions, Ronan Keating, Stephen Gately, Shane Lynch, Mikey Graham and Keith Duffy survived a cull that brought the world Boyzone. Nineteen UK Top Forty singles (including six number ones) later, not to mention countless Top Ten hits in Ireland, and Boyzone became one of the most successful bands in the history of British and Irish pop. By 2010, the band had sold 20 million records, thus making them and their manager very wealthy men.

Not one to miss a trick, Louis was ahead of the curve when he realized that Boyzone were starting to run out of steam. Rather than trying to reinvent the wheel, he simply did the same thing as before only, with the benefit of the Boyzone experience, a little bigger and a lot better. In 1998 Louis conjured up Westlife and record companies fell over themselves to sign the lads. In the end, Simon Cowell did the honours for RCA and so a very important and influential relationship began. Ronan Keating, by now an adult, stepped in as co-manager and Westlife burst on to the scene with 'Swear It Again' (1999), a ballad that summed up the 'sound' that would prove a winning one for the boys, whose next six singles went straight to number one. Under the canny guidance of their manager, Westlife stayed the course in the fickle world of pop music, lasting fourteen years or thereabouts at the top before mounting their stools for their last key-change at a series of emotional farewell concerts in Dublin's Croke Park in the summer of 2012. They'd sold more than 44 million records around the world.

Louis was a Svengali for the first three decades of his career. That all changed in 2001 when he appeared as a judge on the Irish television version of *Popstars*. Initially, he didn't see himself as television material: 'I didn't want to do that show but they offered me a lot of money. It was never in my plan. I didn't want to be on TV.'

As it turned out, he was a natural and within a year was doing the same thing on a different show for more money and to a bigger audience, this time in the UK as a judge on *Popstars: The Rivals*. It is a role that has kept him on the biggest shows on British television ever since. With Simon Cowell by his side, Louis moved seamlessly to *X Factor*, where he remains the only constant in a sea of change.

What has kept him there appears to be a mixture of patronage and pedantry. Described by one journalist as having 'a tongue on him like a fishwife with a bad hangover', Louis has a propensity to call it like it is, regardless of the sensitivities of those at the receiving end of the lash. And so, Robbie Williams is a 'jumped-up karaoke singer, the biggest con artist of all time' and Kylie just happens to be lucky enough to possess 'a great ass and a massively powerful machine behind her'. His acid tongue can be at its most harsh when he is crossed. Such was the case during his acrimonious falling out with Ronan Keating (since resolved). At the time, Louis said that, in Boyzone, Keating 'wasn't the most talented one – he's not a great singer and he's got no personality'. Keating was quick to respond (via a magazine interview) when he said that Louis 'tried to ruin me and if he thinks we can ever hug and make up, he can forget it . . . He's not a nice character.' Apart from that very public falling out, it is rare to see Louis Walsh in a bad light in British or Irish tabloids. A master of the dark arts, his nurturing of media contacts is the stuff of legend and if you see Louis in the papers, it'll most likely be a shot of him arriving at Elton John's latest party with Sharon Osbourne on his arm.

Despite his reputedly vast wealth, Louis' only concessions to expenditure are art (he owns 'Warhol and stuff') and property (he has homes in Ireland, London and Miami), but generally he likes to keep his lifestyle low-key. A regular in Marks & Spencer, the confirmed bachelor admits to having 'lots of acquaintances but I'm lucky if I've got a handful of real friends'. Despite losing €10 million in the property crash, Louis keeps a chipper outlook and the need for a job at McDonald's appears as unlikely as ever.

As for the future? He is stepping down from *X Factor* and going back to managing singers and boy bands, but it seems that Louis' energy is boundless and does not include any plans for pulling back on his workload: 'Retirement? No, that's for the civil service. Because I love what I do, it's not like work to me. If I ever get fed up of doing what I do, I'll retire. I want to keep going and I think there's life in the old dog yet.'

And so, for Louis Walsh, the beat goes on. But sadly it didn't for one of the young lads he discovered . . .

STEPHEN GATELY: reluctant hero

17 March 1976–10 October 2009

> No marching or shouting but Stephen Gately
> was a gay rights hero.
>
> — *The Times*

Boy bands are carefully styled to appeal to young girls (many of them pre-pubescent) with pocket money to spend, but they are also role models for a large number of young boys. And some of these boys will be gay and just taking the first steps towards learning what it means to be gay in a predominantly straight society. That's why it was hugely significant when Stephen Gately of Boyzone 'came out' at the height of his fame in 1999. It doesn't matter that he came out when forced to do so after someone he'd slept with was planning to sell their story to the press. The important thing is that he was honest about it and, if anything, it enhanced the band's following.

Gately grew up in a working-class district of Dublin, the fourth of five children. After school, he worked as a barman and shop assistant until the fateful day in 1993 when he was picked from more than 300 applicants to become a member of Boyzone. The day after the line-up was confirmed they appeared on the *Late Late Show*, where my predecessor Gay Byrne had to work hard to make sense of the boy band concept: 'They don't sing, don't write music, don't play instruments ... they'll go far.' The boys performed a demented dance to an instrumental backing track and it was immediately clear that Gately was by far the best dancer (the lack of competition helped). When they began performing live, he usually shared the lead vocals with Ronan Keating, and his voice rings out on all their hit singles through the six years they topped the charts.

In 2000, the band members decided to part company and focus on solo projects and Gately made an album called *New Beginning* before he was unceremoniously dropped by his record company. It can't have been easy to adjust after all the fame and adulation, and there was a period when he admitted to depression and substance abuse. He picked himself up and found happiness again with his partner Andrew Cowles, whom he 'married' in 2003 at a commitment ceremony in Las Vegas. The couple lived together in north London and talked about possibly having children, while Gately found work on television and in West End shows.

In 2008, Boyzone reformed, did two sell out tours and brought out another album. Gately was riding high once more when tragedy struck while he was on holiday in Majorca with Cowles in October 2009. While sleeping on a sofa in their apartment he died of a pulmonary embolism brought on by an undiagnosed heart condition. Deeply distressed, the four other members of Boyzone flew out to collect his body and brought him back for a celebrity- and fan-packed funeral in Dublin's Church of St Laurence O'Toole.

But Gately was to have one more important influence on the

world. Before the autopsy results were released, a *Daily Mail* columnist wrote a piece questioning why a fit and healthy thirty-three-year-old man would simply die in his sleep and suggesting that drugs and his 'dangerous lifestyle' might be implicated. Such was the ensuing furore that the Press Complaints Commission website crashed with the sheer volume of complaints, and celebrities and journalists alike queued up to condemn the homophobic tone of the piece. *Father Ted* writer Graham Linehan (see Chapter 2) wrote that if Gately's passing 'causes today's kind of gutter-journalism to be held to account, we can perhaps take that as a tribute'. I hope it will make journalists think twice before writing such a thing again.

The world had progressed a lot since 1993, when Gately went to that first life-changing audition. Louis Walsh later admitted that he might not have picked him if he had known about his sexuality at the time, telling the *Irish Times*, 'It wasn't cool then to have a gay guy in a band.' But Gately made it cool and paved the way for later boy band members, such as Mark Feehily of Westlife, to come out. As Gately himself commented, 'It's just me being me and I don't think there should be a real big issue about the whole thing anyway.'

NIALL HORAN: 'the cute one'
Born 13 September 1993

Every now and then you have like a realization moment where you get goosebumps and think, 'I am literally the luckiest person in the world.'

The phone rang in a modest home in Mullingar, County Westmeath. Bobby Horan answered to be told that the band his son was in was en route to the Number One slot in the charts. In the American charts. Bobby, a butcher at the local Tesco, was delighted but life had to go on: 'I was just clocking on for a thirteen-hour night shift. I couldn't believe it . . . but I wasn't going to go home and celebrate – I had a job to do.' This pretty much sums up both father and son's approach to being in one of the biggest pop bands on the planet. Even after a string of number one hits, Niall Horan was home for Christmas, tweeting pictures of himself with friends holding a chicken snack box in the air with some pride. You can take the boy out of Mullingar . . .

Like some other subjects in this book, Niall was educated by the Christian Brothers with their aim of turning out good Catholic boys, but his life changed dramatically when he joined a queue at 5am, in April 2010. The queue was made up of thousands of young hopefuls, hoping to make it into the British television talent show *X Factor*. His audition went well but there was a moment when it looked like he was going to be thrown out of the competition at the early boot-camp stage. That was until the judges brought Niall and four other solo hopefuls back on stage and told them to go off and form a band. They became One Direction and a phenomenon was born. They came third and yet are arguably the most successful act to emerge from the decade-old television show (Matt Cardle won and has hardly been seen since). Hundreds of girls were swarming outside the TV studios hoping for a glimpse of Niall and his bandmates Zayn, Liam, Harry and Louis, and the wily Simon Cowell saw a business opportunity. He signed them up and the band went from hopeful obscurity to international pandemonium at breakneck speed.

In Ireland, they were quick to claim a stake in the pop prize and every time Niall Horan came on the *Late Late Show*, I was happy to focus on the Irish question. Irish people love watching other Irish people on television. All our biggest ratings on the show are for Irish guests rather than international ones. We're intrigued to know what they sound like, what they look like, if they're polite, rude, confident or shy – everything about them. One man's curiosity is another man's nosiness but it was a good, light news story in a sea of gravity: 'Irish boy makes good in the British pop world'.

And make good he certainly did! One Direction's first single, 'What Makes You Beautiful', had the highest number of pre-orders in the history of Sony Records and sold 153,000 copies in just seven days. Since then, One Direction has been on an upward trajectory. Niall Horan appears to be enjoying the meteoric rise as much as his 13.3 million (and growing) Twitter followers, who know what he's watching, where he's eating and who he's dating.

He's moved to London but so that he didn't feel too homesick, he moved Mum in just round the corner. So far it looks as though he's doing just fine in what is called a 'British boy band'. In many respects, that's what they are. Many, but not all . . .

*   *   *

There's a tendency to be sniffy about boy bands in some sectors of the media, with critics saying they're all appearance and no substance. Their music is often created by experienced pop pro-ducers and all they have to do is show up with the right clothes and hairstyles, remember a few dance steps and sing in tune (or mime convincingly). They're supposed to be squeaky clean role models for a generation and most bands have a built-in lifespan and self-destruct when they reach their mid-twenties. However, even if all this were true (and many boy bands transcend the genre expectations), I still say, what's the harm? They're not bad role models for our young boys – and pre-teen girls could choose much worse for their first crushes.

Perhaps there is a danger in the young building up their hopes that fame can be achieved so easily, because that way huge disappointment lies for most. But they're young – they'll get over it in the time it takes to post a new picture on Facebook or figure out the latest Xbox game. In the next chapter we'll be looking at another way a lucky few can leapfrog to stardom – and asking why one of the world's biggest movie franchises has such a strong Celtic connection.

10

THE HARRY POTTER BUNCH

WHILE THE HARRY POTTER BOOKS seem very British on the written page, the movies took on a life of their own with the help of some fine Irish actors who captured the mischief and divilment required to bring otherworldly literary qualities to the big screen. When it comes to casting school-kid characters, especially those found messing down the back of the class rather than paying rapt attention up the front, the movie people often turn to Ireland. Rebellious, full of chat and armed with a bag full of clichés, the Potter people struck gold when they turned their gaze to Ireland. The Irish pretty much supplied half the cast . . .

Richard Harris accepted the role of Dumbledore, head of Hogwarts, in *Harry Potter and the Sorceror's Stone* (2001) not because he was bowled over by the part but because his eleven-year-old granddaughter vowed never to speak to him again if he turned it down! When Harris died in 2002, Michael Gambon donned the wizard's robes and used an Irish lilt in Dumbledore's speech as a mark of respect to his old friend.

Fiona Shaw shone as Harry Potter's aunt Petunia Dursley, the hater of all things wizard- and magic-related, in five of the films.

She is a master of comic timing and expressions of horror when things explode around her house, and they couldn't have picked anyone better to play the narrow-minded, snobbish 'Muggle'.

As with so many Hollywood baddies down through the years, the bad guy with the white kitten or a penchant for violence has an Etonian spoon in his mouth and so the same goes for the Potter bad boys: bleached-blond Tom Felton, who plays Draco Malfoy; Alan Rickman as Professor Severus Snape; Ralph Fiennes as Lord Voldemort. It's rare to find an Irish baddie in any film, and there certainly aren't any in the Harry Potter movies. A lot of the non-Irish goodies have Celtic blood in their veins: Robbie Coltrane as a Scottish Hagrid; Belfast-born Ciarán Hinds, who plays Dumbledore's brother Aberforth; and Rupert Grint as Ron Weasley, who could easily be Irish with that red hair and freckles. The Irish just don't do very good baddies, if you understand me?

The Potter phenomenon has done wonders for children's literature and the movies act as the perfect complement to the written word. The Irish connection is strong and welcome, and this is how we contributed to the magic . . .

BRENDAN GLEESON: the crazy mad-eyed teacher
Born 29 March 1955

It's the parents that spot me and drag their poor kids over! You can see it in their faces, 'Why am I being introduced to this overweight, middle-aged, very ordinary man?' And of course, without the eye thing, I'm a complete disappointment to them.

Two things strike me whenever I meet and interview Brendan Gleeson. One is his size. Unlike most stars of the big screen, Gleeson is as big and broad as he looks. He has an imposing, physical bulk that has contributed greatly to the type of role he gets in movies and it's the same in any given green room he inhabits. You couldn't miss him.

The second thing that intrigues me is that you'd think he would be brash, a bit loud and a little domineering but he is none of those things. In fact, he's quite the opposite. Low-key, unaffected and borderline shy, Gleeson is the opposite to most of his on-screen personas. I interviewed him with Colin Farrell back in 2008 to discuss *In Bruges*. They are both very gentlemanly (despite media reports to the contrary) and Gleeson pretty much gave Farrell the floor. But in another interview (not my show this time), I heard Gleeson let rip about Ireland's Health Service Executive and he caused quite a stir with his denunciation of that institution. I welcomed him on to the stage the evening Dublin welcomed President Obama in 2011 and again Gleeson gave a charged speech, urging the assembled crowd to stop gazing at their shoes and to look up and look forward. He was angry and wanted to promote hope. This is the house style of the man: reticent yet passionate, high profile but low maintenance, big star with little ego.

Born into the post-Emergency period, Gleeson joined an austere Dublin that lacked great colour or hope. Dad was a civil servant and Mum stopped working in a shoe shop to stay at home with the children. They were book-friendly folks who read to feed their son's curiosity, which was strong enough for him to devour Joyce, Beckett and Faulkner as a teenager. Pat Grogan, a Christian Brother at Gleeson's school, brought drama, theatre and passion to the classroom and beyond and was a critical influence on the young Gleeson. The acting bug bit deep and, on leaving school, Gleeson started a drama group and, with it, fired a lifelong interest in the craft.

Long before Harry Potter was a twinkle in J.K. Rowling's eye, Gleeson was working as a teacher, and he was a man on a mission. A young man with a ready-made audience every morning, he saw the job as a calling: 'I was vocational about it . . . teaching's very like acting. With both, you're trying to explore a certain amount of truth and communicate it to people.' His description of those classroom years makes him come across as a working-class version of *Dead Poets' Society* with boys from poorer parts of Dublin encouraged to step outside their comfort zones and embrace difference. Stage shows and annual pageants were the order of the day for Gleeson, who fondly remembers the benign mortification he encouraged: 'There were these fairly tough guys coming out and singing Christmas carols – their cheeks bright red – and I started laughing and couldn't stop. They were looking at me laughing and it was killing them. They'll probably tell me I traumatised them for life.'

Beyond the school walls, Gleeson was pursuing his serious hobby and when he was nominated for a theatre award, he felt it was time to abandon the blackboard and follow his heart. By now he was thirty-four, married with four children and lucky enough to have a secure job. At this stage of his life, it was high-stakes stuff but a decision had to be made: 'I'd always said to myself, I didn't want to get to 35 and have any regrets about my life . . . It felt like someone was knocking on my window and asking me, "What more do you need to take the jump?"' And with that, Brendan Gleeson went home for dinner with his wife, Mary, and it was agreed that acting would now be responsible for putting bread on the table . . .

Luckily for Gleeson, it was 1989 and the Irish film industry was about to enter a purple patch. Theatre work was easily found and the natural progression was onto television where, in 1991, he played Irish revolutionary icon Michael Collins in *The Treaty*. Bit parts in big films followed (*Far and Away*, *Into the West* and *The Snapper*) but he really burst on to the screen as lovable, long-haired twit Hamish in Mel Gibson's *Braveheart* (1995).

Following warm praise for his *Braveheart* appearance, he decided to give Hollywood a shot. A meeting was arranged with an agent who chatted with Gleeson for a while before surmising that he was 'too fat, too old and not good-looking enough' for the Hollywood Hills. Harsh and not true but as Gleeson later reflected, 'At least it was given to me straight between the eyes. I thought, "Right pal, I'll see you at the Oscars."' This story has a happy ending but we'll wait a few paragraphs before we get there . . .

There was plenty of work back in Ireland anyway and countless films followed: a supporting role in Neil Jordan's *Michael Collins* (1996); starring alongside Richard Harris in *Trojan Eddie* (1996); a priest in *The Butcher Boy* (1997), a gangster in *The General* (1998), and before long he was back in the United States (despite the dire prediction) playing alongside Tom Cruise in *Mission: Impossible II* (2000). Gleeson's role sizes were increasing thanks to leading turns in *28 Days Later* (2002) and *Gangs of New York* (2002). He repeatedly surprises with his choice of parts and it is a tribute to his extraordinary versatility that he has ended up in everything from *Troy* (2004) to *The Village* (2004) and on to *Kingdom of Heaven* (2005).

We've got this far and not a wizard in sight but that's about to change. If there were ever going to be a crazy, one-eyed, red-haired lunatic commanding a blackboard at a school for wizards, few would have predicted it would be Brendan Gleeson. In 'real life', he likes to keep himself to himself, but on stage and on screen, another persona appears and commands our attention because, although he doesn't seek it, Gleeson certainly knows how to hold it.

So in 2005, Brendan was driving along with his sons in the car. The phone rang and he pulled in to take the call. The boys watched their dad, who nodded and smiled and promised to call back with a decision. When he hung up, he explained to the gang that he had just been offered the part of Alastor 'Mad-Eye' Moody, Professor of Defence Against the Dark Arts in *Harry Potter and the Goblet of Fire*. The reaction was such that his mind was made up there and then: 'The car erupted in cheers when my boys heard. There was no question, you have to do this, so that's why I got into it.' Once again, Gleeson was in a school, surrounded by children, 'only this time I could do it with magical powers and no conscience!'

He loved the experience on set: 'The kids were allowed to be kids and there was huge respect for the audiences and the people who loved them – there was magic about it that was irreplaceable.' The magic translated at the box office as the Harry Potter series went on to become one of the most lucrative in cinema history. Fortunately for Gleeson, Mad-Eye was to return in *Harry Potter and the Order of the Phoenix* (2007) and three years later in *Harry Potter and the Deathly Hallows: Part 1* (2010).

Beyond the world of Hogwarts, Gleeson was dazzling audiences in comedies like *In Bruges* (2008) and historical roles as Churchill in *Into the Storm* (2009). It's the latter role that brings us to an elevator in a Los Angeles hotel. Gleeson had just been awarded an Emmy for his performance as Britain's wartime leader. As he looked around the enclosed space, he spotted the agent who had assured him that age, looks and weight would end his ambition to be an actor. Many would have held the award close to the man's face by way of lusty revenge but Gleeson smiles at the memory, admitting that he kept his 'mother's dignity' and remained silent. A class act.

DOMHNALL GLEESON: like father, like son

Born 12 May 1983

> I get asked to give stuff to my dad. I'm, like, 'I'm not gonna pass your script to him!' You know? My dad's my dad. I'm not his agent.

At just twelve years old, Domhnall Gleeson nearly starred in a blockbuster movie with his dad. It was *Braveheart* and they were looking for someone to play Brendan Gleeson's character, Hamish Campbell, as a boy. They asked Brendan if he had any sons and Domhnall was duly sent to meet the casting director, who told the youngster that while he was the right age, he just didn't look enough like his father – and so he lost out on a wonderful opportunity.

Less than ten years later, the Harry Potter machine was firing on all cylinders and Domhnall auditioned unsuccessfully for the part of Stan Shunpike, conductor of the Knight Bus in *Harry Potter and the Prisoner of Azkaban*. The following year he tried for the role of Cedric Diggory in *Harry Potter and the Goblet of Fire*. If he had got that part, he would have been in his first Potter film at the same time as his dad – but it went to Robert Pattinson instead.

Thankfully, the producers eventually knocked on Domhnall's door when casting the part of red-haired Weasley sibling Bill in the *Deathly Hallows* two-parter. It was a nervous time for Domhnall, who remembers: 'Joining *Harry Potter* for the first time, I was nearly wetting myself with fear, I was close to needing a bag. It was incredibly scary.' But it all went well in the end with Domhnall revelling in the fact that he had to announce the death of Mad-Eye in the film: '[It] was kind of cool. I got to shout "Mad-Eye is dead!" and you don't get to do that every day.'

Having been a little reluctant to act on screen with his dad ('I thought I'd always have the father-son thing of "He got you the part", which is why Potter didn't seem a good move in that respect') Domhnall now leaps at the chance to act with Brendan: 'You know you have your top ten list of people you want to work with? Well, Dad would be on that list always, regardless if he was my father or not.'

Since his adventures on Planet Potter, Domhnall's fortunes have continued to soar with stellar turns in *Never Let Me Go* (2010), *True Grit* (2010) and *Anna Karenina* (2012), and he remains level-headed in the extreme when it comes to the kind of roles he fully expects to be offered in the future: 'I don't think Colin [Farrell] or Jonathan [Rhys Myers] have to worry about me coming along to steal their Hollywood crown. Nobody's going to offer me a perfume deal or fashion campaign. I mean, they can if they want to, I'm more than happy to endorse the latest fragrance with my top off, looking all pasty and bloated and out of shape, but somehow I think they'd always go for someone who looks like those two. But you never know, my look could become the latest trend and suddenly I'll be flooded with offers. Maybe Colin and Jonathan should be worried after all.'

Domhnall was one of my first guests on the autumn 2013 *Late Late Show*. Growing in confidence but retaining his trademark shyness, he laughed off suggestions that he was the next Hugh Grant. He had to deny it because every paper that week accused him of being very Grant-y in *About Time*, the film that has brought Domhnall to a rom-com audience and, with it, a further step up the ladder.

At the end of our interview, I alluded to the fact that Bob Geldof was standing nearby getting ready to sing with the Boomtown Rats. I reminded Domhnall that he had played Bob in a drama once. Geldof heard the exchange and shouted over, 'Yeah, he was shite!' Domhnall burst out laughing while repeating what Bob had said but quickly reminding us that he was on the chat show to raise funds for a hospice, concluding his appearance with the words, 'Just give us your money, Bob.' It was a clever reference to Geldof's Live Aid plea and immediately drew laughs from the audience. Life and art collided that night.

If there was an international pictorial dictionary that showed a face for each country, Domhnall's could easily appear under 'Ireland'. Red-haired, freckled and self-deprecating to a fault, young Gleeson is swiftly emerging from his father's shadow and I suspect he will go a long, long way. Magic.

DEVON MURRAY: playing dumb

28 October 1988

> It's not like I try to blow things up, exactly, it just sorta happens. You gotta admit, though, fire is fascinating.
> – Devon Murray as Seamus Finnigan

Devon Murray's voice hadn't broken when he was cast as Harry Potter's clumsy Irish pal in Hogwarts. Born in County Kildare, Devon was a lovely surprise for his parents, who had given up hope of having children until their little boy arrived out of the blue in 1988 (feeling old anyone?). He hasn't stopped surprising them ever since.

An active child with a cheeky grin, he attended stage school in Dublin and graduated to the National Performing Arts Stage School. Devon's pre-Potter appearances on screen were brief and involved ads for Tesco and Dulux paint as well as playing young Malachy McCourt, Frank's brother, in *Angela's Ashes* (1999).

The big moment came when Devon successfully auditioned for the part of Seamus Finnigan in *Harry Potter and the Sorcerer's Stone*, which came out in 2001. It was a plum role that kept Devon busy for the next ten years and saw him in all eight of the Potter films. Not everyone was happy with the idea of an Irish lad being cast as the slightly thick magician in the class (Devon says of Seamus: 'My character's a bit stupid, he can't get anything right, especially magic homework'). Being honest, I groaned when I saw Seamus Finnigan appear on the cinema screen with his freckles and foolish grin. I felt it was pretty retrograde for such a smart author to write a dumb Irish character. Am I falling into the 'hyper-sensitive' trap? Possibly, but as a country replete with Nobel Prize winners, I thought we deserved a little better than this glib characterization. Rant over. At least we got Dumbledore!

The commitment required for the Potter movies was enormous. At one point, Devon was asked to play the young Leonardo DiCaprio in *Gangs of New York* but couldn't because of his part with Potter. In other words, at just thirteen years old Devon Murray was saying 'no' to Martin Scorcese!

By the time Brendan Gleeson arrived on set to play Mad-Eye Moody in *Harry Potter and the Goblet of Fire*, Devon was the Potter veteran to Brendan's rookie. The teenager welcomed his compatriot:

'I took him under my wing and showed him the ropes because I worked with everyone and he was the new guy.'

A fan of horses and cars since he was a child, Devon has amassed fame and fortune thanks to his ten years in Potterville, but he says he hasn't changed a bit: 'I'm still plain old Devon. I love horse riding, playing my computer, roller blades and skate board.' But it's the caveat that reveals a material change in the former magician: 'I'm a rich man now, I've got enough to buy a car.'

EVANNA LYNCH: the hippy dippy one
Born 16 August 1991

I saw her. [She] got in my head. I even heard her voice when I was writing Luna.

> – J.K. Rowling on Evanna Lynch

Evanna Lynch looks at photographs of herself as a young girl these days and laughs. There she is, in full school uniform, asleep with a copy of *Harry Potter* dropped beside her when she could read no more due to exhaustion. The adventures of J.K. Rowling's plucky magician were an obsession for the girl from Termonfeckin who started writing to the author when she was eleven. In one of those letters Evanna told Rowling that she wanted to act in a Potter film one day but doubted this could happen for a girl from a sleepy town in County Louth. Within weeks, Evanna received a letter from the Potter creator in which she wrote: 'Don't be too hard on Termonfeckin; it does have a brilliant name! And I come from a very sleepy place.'

After this, the letters came and went between the two new pen pals. It was a tough time for Evanna, who had an eating disorder and was struggling with low confidence. Throughout this time, Rowling encouraged her and when Evanna expressed an interest in acting in a Potter film, the author told her: 'You need to be well first, you need to be comfortable with yourself.' It was this kind of guidance that Evanna is certain helped her to recover.

It was enough to build Evanna's confidence and when an ad was posted looking for kids to audition for the part of dreamy-hippy magician Luna Lovegood, Evanna convinced her dad to take her to London to have a go. They'd tried casting Luna in stage schools but that proved fruitless so there was to be an open, public audition. Evanna went along and within a week was called to read for the part in a screen test. She was pitched against Daniel Radcliffe for this element of the process and three days later, following a gruelling trawl that involved more than 15,000 girls, the movie people had found their Luna in Evanna Lynch from Termonfeckin.

Having seen her audition for the part, one of the producers, David Heyman, said: 'The others could play Luna; Evanna Lynch is Luna.' The two aren't dissimilar in many respects: Evanna exudes a dreamlike quality that gives her an ethereal, otherworldly vibe. She says of her alter ego: 'I don't think she's weird, she's completely herself. She's OK with being eccentric and a little different.' That could be a description of Evanna herself; she does admit there are similarities between the two personas right down to a shared taste in kooky clothes. When producers couldn't decide on a hat for Luna to wear at a Quidditch match, they asked Evanna to dream something up and it is her design that she wears as she shouts for Gryffindor in *Harry Potter and the Half Blood Prince* (2009).

Like the other Irish Harry Potter actors (apart from Fiona Shaw), she played Luna Lovegood with a bit of brogue: 'I love that

I get to keep my Irish accent in my films – and I think that's really important, it is to me.'

When the film series came to an end, Evanna did things she couldn't do while involved in the world of Potter, such as dyeing her hair red, 'getting braces on my teeth, learning to drive a car and being with friends in one place for a fixed set of time'. She has also modelled for photo shoots, done charity work and will be seen in other acting roles before long. Termonfeckin should be very proud!

*   *   *

It's a shame they didn't film any of the *Harry Potter* movies in Ireland. J.K. Rowling's Scottish homeland got the honour when they needed to show the train journey to Hogwarts, but I'd like to send her a personal message that the Irish would offer a warm welcome to any more films she cares to write. Acclaimed TV series *Ripper Street* is being shot in Dublin and I hear whispers of a lot of filming going on out here just now, so maybe there's a halcyon period on the way.

Meanwhile, there's another movie franchise with an Irish connection that has so far produced twenty-three movies compared to *Harry Potter*'s eight. The films have been shot in more than fifty countries, and eight different actors have played the lead character. And it could have been an Irish franchise had things gone a little differently. In that case, the well-known catchphrase might have been 'O'Bond. The name's Seamus O'Bond.'

11

THE
JAMES BOND
FRANCHISE

I've always loved Bond. The action, the adventure, the cocktails, the sinuous women and the men with metal instead of teeth! What's not to love? In a world without laptops, iPads and mobile phones, families used to sit on the couch every Sunday afternoon and watch any Bond movie that took a scheduler's fancy. Moody Sean, cheeky Roger, intense Timothy, tuxedo-clad while gambling and knocking back martinis and planning the next conquest, be they villain or sultry beauty.

For me as a growing boy, Bond was quintessentially British. Given my childhood was set against the backdrop of Cold War politics, James was invariably up against another Englishman playing a Russian with a dubious but generic 'Eastern' accent that did the job. I never realized there was anything Irish about the Bond movies, but I'd have been delighted if I had. And an Irishman playing Bond? That would have been my dream.

If you can believe a story Michael Gambon tells, it almost happened in the late 60s. Gambon fully acknowledges that he isn't heart-throb material but claims he nonetheless got a call from James Bond producer Albert 'Cubby' Broccoli. Gambon showed up at the Mayfair office as instructed, accepted both a salmon sandwich and a glass of champagne, before Broccoli explained the nature of the meeting. 'We're looking for a new James Bond,' he announced. Gambon nearly choked on his salmon and started laughing before asking incredulously, 'James Bond? Me? I'm not the right shape!' But Broccoli was insistent: 'We have ice bags for Sean's chest which we put on just before a take to shrink him in . . . Teeth? Well, we can do that in an afternoon . . . And I'll get a toupee for you.' The lunch concluded, the two men shook hands but Gambon was never offered the role. If, indeed, the meeting took place at all – which I'll leave up to you to decide.

It was after I left school and began work as a cub reporter that I first came across an Irish connection with the legendary action franchise, and then some years after that when I discovered that the whole Bond œuvre could have been Irish productions, give or take a few little lawsuits and umpteen paragraphs of legalese fine print . . .

KEVIN McCLORY: the litigious writer/producer
8 June 1926–20 November 2006

> The Bond movies have made so much money that these legal actions have become endemic, but for me, it's just a temporary nuisance.

Kevin McClory was everything that Ian Fleming was not. The Irishman wasn't born into the rarefied world of Oxbridge literary otherworldliness but rather bounced into Dublin in 1926 with a cruel irony that saw him related to the Brontës and yet suffering from severe dyslexia at school.

While Ian Fleming swept through the corridors of Foreign Office power, McClory was on a ship in the merchant navy dreaming of becoming an actor. The vessel was torpedoed in 1943, resulting in him acquiring a stammer that forced a rethink of his post-war plans.

After the war, while Ian Fleming tapped away at his typewriter, deep in his enormously successful series of James Bond books, McClory got a job as a dogsbody at Shepperton Studios, working as a boom operator or making tea for more important people.

Learning fast and employing a cocky way with words that endeared him to some but turned others off, McClory caught the attention of the iconic film director John Huston, who took the young Irishman on as his assistant in movies like *The African Queen* and *Moulin Rouge* before eventually making him assistant director on *Moby Dick* in 1956.

Always ambitious, McClory struck out on his own in 1959 when he wrote, produced and directed *The Boy and the Bridge*. At around this time, he befriended Ivar Bryce, a wealthy Englishman who helped finance the Irishman's first film outing. Bryce was a close friend of Fleming's and the two men's paths crossed as Bryce urged McClory to read the Bond novels with a view to bringing them to the big screen. McClory loved the books but felt they needed more drama and action so he suggested that he, along with Fleming and Bryce, should bring in a screenwriter to help create a Bond adventure purpose-built for the cinema. Jack Whittingham became the fourth member of this Bond band, a first draft was written, a name was bestowed upon it and *Thunderball* was born – and with it came a legal s**tstorm that would last for decades.

The trouble really started when Fleming and Bryce got cold feet and abandoned the project – and McClory with it. But while they might have left McClory, McClory wasn't about to leave them.

By 1961, Ian Fleming was fifty-three years old and the ideas just weren't coming in the way they used to. In a letter to an old military friend, Fleming wrote: 'What was easy at 40 is very difficult at 50. I used to believe sufficiently in Bonds and blondes and bombs. Now the keys creak as I type and I fear the zest may have gone.'

Maybe it was his diminishing literary mojo, maybe it was laziness or maybe it was out and out plagiarism that led Fleming simply to lift his next story from the *Thunderball* script without asking either Whittingham or McClory for their permission, and that was his biggest mistake. Time to call in the lawyers.

Late in 1963, London's High Court played host to the Bond trial. Nine days into the trial, Fleming (and Bryce) decided to settle with McClory. Ian Fleming could keep ownership of the *Thunderball* novel but all future editions would include the sub-heading 'Based on a screen treatment by Kevin McClory, Jack Whittingham and the author'. McClory was granted 'the exclusive right to use James Bond as a character in any such scripts or film of *Thunderball*'.

McClory was happy with the outcome, repairing to a nearby pub with his wife and his friend Peter O'Toole. Who else?

At this stage, there had been three Bond movies and what would become known as 'branding' was having its effect at the box office. For McClory to make a Bond film without the familiar theme music, gun barrel opening and one Sean Connery would be odd and unlikely to wash with cinemagoers, so an alliance would have to be formed between the Irishman and the Bond big guns, Broccoli and Saltzman. They weren't too keen on another Bond franchise emerging to dilute the power of their 007 but in September 1964,

Albert 'Cubby' Broccoli and Harry Saltzman landed in Dublin where they met McClory and agreed to make *Thunderball* together. Credits-wise, McClory was producer, while Broccoli and Saltzman got the executive producer title. The result was box-office gold with takings in excess of $140 million.

Kevin McClory moved back to Ireland and bought a magnificent estate in County Kildare that would later become the world-famous K Club golf course. Aside from messy legal battles, little was heard from him until 1983. That year is significant because it marked the end of a restriction that had been imposed on McClory preventing him from making any further films based on the *Thunderball* film material. To get another Bond movie of any credibility made, McClory needed a trump card. Enter stage left, Sean Connery.

The Scotsman had retired from the Bond series in 1971 after *Diamonds Are Forever*. McClory had remained good friends with Connery and knew of his interest in flexing his artistic muscle. Sensing an opportunity, McClory offered Connery a writing credit but also proposed that he might dust down his tuxedo one last time. Dividing their time between Ireland and Connery's Marbella home, the two men together with the writer Len Deighton wrote a script with a working title of 'James Bond of the Secret Service'. This was changed to *Warhead* and this in turn became *Never Say Never Again* (referring to the fact that Connery had already retired as Bond twice!).

It was twelve years since the world had seen Connery as 007 and the result was a resounding success. *Never Say Never Again* raked in $160 million worldwide.

There was some talk in the 90s that McClory was going to make yet another reworking of the *Thunderball* script with a working title of *Warhead 2000AD* but nothing came of it.

Fond of a drink, one report suggests that McClory was at one stage drinking a bottle of Jack Daniels daily. He often hung out with Peter O'Toole and Richard Harris, and in 1975 he and Harris followed in a long line of artists sticking their nose into politics when he took out a newspaper advert demanding an end to internment without trial in Northern Ireland. It didn't go down too well with the British political establishment, but that wouldn't have bothered these two staunch nationalists.

McClory tried one last lawsuit, claiming that he was the co-author of the 007 seen on screen and should be paid for *all* the films, but this was thrown out of court. It does make you think, though. What if he hadn't fallen out with Ian Fleming over *Thunderball*? He could have been writer/producer of the entire series of Bond films and maybe, just maybe, he would have brought them home to Ireland. We can but dream.

MARTIN GRACE: all because the lady loves

12 September 1942–27 January 2010

> The bravest man I've ever known.
>
> – Roger Moore

Some years ago, as a rookie reporter on Irish radio, I was given the chance to spend a summer doing things that were alien to me. So for a number of weeks I learned different skills and reported on my success or otherwise at the end of each week. I tried my hand at stand-up comedy, opera singing, football commentary, hairdressing, auctioneering and, most memorably for me, learning to be a stuntman. Given my slight physique, this was hilarious in itself. At the end of 'stunt week' I was to be set alight and thrown down a flight of concrete steps. Easy.

Each of these tasks required me to seek out a mentor and after a quick search around for famous Irish stuntmen, I found a very humble yet robust County Kilkenny man called Martin Grace. With great skill and considerable tenacity, Martin took me through the motions and, as we spent time self-immolating and performing other random acts of violence, we became friends. When we weren't recording clips for the radio show, he filled me in on his life story and now I'd like to share that exciting adventure with you.

When a travelling cinema tent pitched up in a small Irish village early in the 1950s, little did they know that sitting in the audience, wide-eyed and mesmerized by the cowboys flickering before him, was a boy who would become one of the great stuntmen of his generation. More travelling shows visited Martin Grace's village of Lisdowney and each one pushed him further towards the path that would take him all the way to the Golden Gate Bridge, where he eventually ended up as the 'hidden' James Bond.

When attending point-to-point races at Balleen, the young Martin saw a man who balanced a bicycle and a ladder on his chin. There was a monkey on top of the ladder, and Martin was agog. Always an active child in school, he was the go-to guy when a ball flew over the wall. One of his teachers felt Martin could have been a sports star, maybe playing for his native Kilkenny, but it wasn't to be. Ireland in the 50s was defined by austerity and emigration and for Martin, the mix of glamour and sporting endeavour was a calling and only one city would cater for such needs: 'Emigration at that time seemed an attractive option and London was near and there was lots more happening there at that time regarding sports facilities and entertainment.'

A brief stint selling cars was followed by a more appropriate starter job as a Redcoat in Butlin's, where Martin put his gym-honed physique to good use, organizing sports days and appearing on stage by night – the perfect combination for an aspiring stunt-man.

Nineteen sixty-four was an important year for Martin Grace largely thanks to the fact that a certain woman really loved a particular brand of chocolate. Action movies were all the rage and the marketing people at Cadburys leaped at the idea of showing a shadowy figure emerging from all sorts of adventurous and unlikely scenarios to deliver a box of Milk Tray to a woman who was as beautiful as she was grateful. Martin was required to leap on to the roof of a moving train, pull himself from a sports car up into a helicopter, dive on to a speeding truck and swing across a vast gorge while being chased by wolves in order to leave the box of chocolates and his card in the lady's bedroom to the voiceover 'All because the lady loves . . . Milk Tray.'

Thankfully, it wasn't only ladies who enjoyed that ad. The stunt coordinator of the James Bond films had seen Martin's work in the Milk Tray ads and asked him to join the crew on *You Only Live Twice* (1967), a movie that required lots of stuntmen to slide down ropes and leap off hidden trampolines for the 'I've just been blown away by a bomb' effect. After a month training for the part, Martin got stuck in and began an association with the Bond franchise that would go on for six more films.

Roger Moore never pretended to be a real-life action man and had a lot of time for Martin, who became his stunt alter ego, starting with *The Man with the Golden Gun* in 1974. Martin rode camels for Moore in *The Spy Who Loved Me* (1977), was involved in the dramatic opening helicopter scene in *For Your Eyes Only*

(1981) and featured in *Moonraker* (1979) and *Octopussy* (1983), while perhaps saving his most daring and iconic scenes for *A View to a Kill* (1985), in which Martin can be spotted (especially if you're quick with the 'pause' button) replacing Moore on the Golden Gate Bridge and the Eiffel Tower. They only got permission to do the high-risk Golden Gate Bridge stunt on the understanding that there would be no actual fighting! And the high-speed car chase on location in Sardinia for *The Spy Who Loved Me* came with a special challenge when Martin was told that he was to return the Lotus Esprit without a scratch or a bump because it had to be returned to the showroom blemish-free.

Martin got on particularly well with Richard Kiel, the seven-foot-two actor who played Jaws in *The Spy Who Loved Me* and *Moonraker*, for whom he occasionally stood in. Whereas Kiel found it hard wearing a set of metal teeth for the role, spitting them out as soon as the director shouted 'Cut!', Martin rather resourcefully wore pieces of orange peel wrapped in tinfoil. When he was asked about Kiel by schoolchildren, Martin explained that in real life, Jaws was 'very feeble, has back and neck problems. We rehearsed him coming after me. I vault over some rails to escape him as he grabs me and he is meant to drag me back over the rail like a rag doll. I have my left hand on the rail and as he attempts to lift me, I help him by pushing down on the bar and vaulting back over. He is one of the nicest and kindest people you could ever meet.'

Martin had a close call while filming *Octopussy* in 1982. In one scene, he is hanging from a moving train but during filming, the train overshot its track. Martin was facing the opposite way and slammed into a wall. Among many other injuries, he broke his pelvis. Looking back on the accident Martin recalled: 'The impact was so lightning fast that I only realized I had hit something when

I found I was hanging prone for dear life on the side of the train. I looked down and saw my trouser leg had been ripped off and saw my thighbone through the gash in my thigh muscle. The train came to a stop, I still hung on miraculously.'

Martin spent several months in hospital but returned to work and went on to work as a stunt double or stunt coordinator on films ranging from *Indiana Jones* to *The Truman Show* and *Saving Private Ryan*.

I recall as if it were yesterday the morning Martin set me on fire and threw me down those concrete steps. Apart from the queue of people trying to help him, I remember most Martin's calm and very cool professionalism. Everything was done by the book but he put me at ease by laughing along the way. He decided that he should use the *Cool Hand Luke* line 'What we have here is a failure to communicate', which he uttered before producing the box of matches. Oddly, I wasn't as nervous as I should've been and that is only because of Martin, whose surname was profoundly well deserved.

'I never felt a stunt was scary,' he said. 'As a professional stunt person, if you are scared then you should not be there . . . we are expected to instil calm.'

Sadly, Martin passed away at the age of sixty-seven following a cycling accident in Spain. He was buried in the family grave at home in Freshford, and among those paying tribute to him was Sir Roger Moore, the man for whom he had so often thrown himself into the line of cinematic danger.

PIERCE BROSNAN: the smooth operator

Born 16 May 1953

> [Brosnan] slots so naturally into the role of James Bond
> one assumes his mother bottle-fed him on vodka martinis
> and his pram came equipped with rocket launchers.
>
> — Peter Carrick, *Pierce Brosnan*

Watching Bond from my couch in the Dublin suburbs, I could understand how a Scot like Connery got the job or how two terribly English men like Moore and Dalton got the nod. (Lazenby, the Australian, continues to baffle Bond fans so we'll just motor on.) What I often wondered was – could an Irishman ever play the most British of all Her Majesty's secret servants? As the 80s progressed, more and more eyes were turning towards a dark and brooding young man who was making a name for himself in America. The show was *Remington Steele*, the man was Brosnan, Pierce Brosnan (sorry).

It was a stormy night in Drogheda when Tom and May Brosnan brought their son Pierce into the world. Nine months earlier, to the very day, the Brosnans had got married. This May evening was one of last times the three would be together as a family because Tom was nearly twice May's age when the pair married and it wasn't long before they realized how little they had in common. Soon after Pierce was born, Tom packed his bags and left for England. When Pierce was a little boy, his mother also left him behind to make a better life for herself and, she hoped, her son, by pursuing a career in London as a nurse.

Abandoned by both parents, Pierce was delivered into the loving arms of his maternal grandparents in County Meath, who adored the boy in return. But by the time Pierce was six, both grandparents were dead and he was on the move again, this time to his mother's great aunt Eileen, with whom he lived for five years.

In between all this disorder, Pierce Brosnan recalls his experience at a strict Christian Brothers school where the men in black were 'dreadful human beings . . . and the cruelness of their ways towards children. They were very sexually repressed. It was ugly. I learnt nothing from the Christian Brothers – except shame.' His childhood memories are predominantly melancholic: 'My life in Ireland was very solitary and there was a lot of loneliness. I felt like an outsider. I felt different.'

Not long after his eleventh birthday, Pierce was plucked from the quiet roads and green fields of Navan, County Meath, handed holy water in an aspirin bottle and a string of rosary beads and sent to join his mother in London. Pierce claims, 'The day I departed – August 12th 1964 – was the very same day Bond's creator Ian Fleming died.' If this was the case, it began a bizarre and mutually beneficial relationship between the handsome young Irish boy with the complicated past and the secret agent who would come to loom large in Pierce's life.

Having felt like an outsider in his own hometown, Pierce landed in London bewildered by his new set-up: 'When I arrived I somehow knew I was going to be different from the other boys back home in County Meath. If I look at my life as a play, Ireland was the first act – my spirit and soul are Irish – and London was the second.'

Not the most academic kid in the class, Pierce learned how to survive the rough and tumble that was involved in being an Irish boy in Putney: 'I got ribbed a lot because of my very strong Irish accent and was nicknamed "Irish". I think the way the English make fun of the Irish is unfortunate. But I was also painfully shy.'

The local cinema in Putney would open Pierce's eyes to a universe of possibilities. Sure, he had seen plenty of films in Ireland but they were black-and-white Norman Wisdom comedies or run-of-the-mill Westerns. In Putney, he sat down to watch *Goldfinger*, the new James Bond adventure, in glorious Technicolor, and it took his breath away: 'I looked up at the big screen . . . and saw a naked lady painted in gold and a cool man who could get out of any situation. I was captivated, magicked, blown away. It stirred things in my loins I had never known before! "Wow," I thought. "I wish I was James Bond!"'

It would be tempting to finish here as you all know the outcome but the road to Bondville was to be complicated and chaotic.

On leaving school, Pierce got involved with a theatre outfit called Oval House, a place that had given the world Steven Berkoff and Tim Roth. The young Irishman found acting a form of emotional release: 'I could act out all the stuff from my childhood; I could let it all out and just go mad. It was brilliant.'

At the age of twenty-five, Pierce fell very heavily in love with actress Cassie Harris, a separated mother of two who was ten years his senior and the former wife of Dermot Harris, brother of Richard. They were married in 1980. The pair were inseparable, with Pierce taking on the father figure role with gusto. He would later adopt the two children when their father died. He had found a family unit at last and was determined to keep it close and tight.

Cassie got a small part in *For Your Eyes Only*, in which she played Countess Lisl von Schlaf. She and Pierce attended the premiere in London where Cassie introduced her husband to Bond supremo, the producer, 'Cubby' Broccoli. It was another domino to fall on that fateful road to *GoldenEye*.

Pierce started to break through in the early 1980s with bit parts in *The Long Good Friday* and *The Mirror Crack'd* as well as a big role in the Irish-American miniseries *The Manions of America* (1981).

It all kicked off in earnest when the family flew out to America. In order to raise money for their tickets, Pierce went to his bank manager, pretended he needed £2,000 to install central heating and spent the money on flights to the United States. He explains, 'Either I stayed in England and worked as a mini-cab driver between the few acting jobs I was being offered or I took a gamble.' The taxi world's loss was the acting world's gain as the gamble paid off and he got an audition for a new TV series. Channelling his inner John Cleese, Cary Grant and James Bond, Pierce landed the role of Remington Steele, a post he would hold for five years and ninety-four episodes. It would be the making but almost the breaking of his bid to be Bond.

It was no great surprise when, after thirteen years and seven movies playing James Bond, Roger Moore decided to hand in his Walther PPK and hang up his eyebrows. Immediately, the spotlight moved across the Atlantic to the *Remington Steele* set. The show had just been cancelled and the thirty-three-year-old Pierce Brosnan could almost taste the bubbles popping in the glass of Dom Perignon. Screen tests, meetings and great excitement ensued until, in the summer of 1986, 'Cubby' Broccoli offered Pierce Brosnan the part he was born to play. The Irishman readily agreed to be the next James Bond and was swiftly sent to the tailor, where he was fitted out in a pristine tuxedo ready to pose on the 007 soundstage at Pinewood studios. It was perfect. In fact, it was too perfect.

In an office far, far away, somebody was reading the small print in Pierce's *Remington Steele* contract. The studio had sixty days to save the series and an option to keep Pierce. The Bond hype had lifted his profile and stock. On the fifty-ninth day, the *Remington Steele* people demanded Pierce make six new episodes of the cancelled series (Broccoli was okay with this) but they also wanted the option of keeping him for a further twenty-two. Game over.

The tuxedo was returned, the announcement withdrawn. Pierce was not going to be James Bond. This time. He returned to the States, made the six episodes and the series was cancelled. Pierce was furious: 'I felt very manipulated and impotent. I never thought I'd get a chance at Bond again. I kissed it goodbye.'

Already feeling angry and dejected, he found out in December 1987 that his beloved Cassie had ovarian cancer. 'Life turned around on a dime,' he reflected.

> She never wanted to die – no one wants to die. And we never talked about it until near the end. I remember one day I was in the studio, painting, and I could hear her down in the kitchen on the phone to the doctor, and I just kept on painting, kept on painting, don't think, don't think. And she came up and she walked behind me and sat down, and I was painting away, just . . . and I said, 'Are you alright?' and she said 'it doesn't look too good for me.' Those were the first heavy words spoken by her. And we just sat there and held each other and wept, and then it was 'OK, right, let's have some lunch . . .' – What else can you talk about?

For four years the pair fought Cassie's illness with everything they had but it proved unstoppable, and on the morning of 28 December 1991, she died in Pierce's arms.

Pierce was on his own for three years before meeting Keely Shaye Smith, an American environmentalist he would marry in

2001. There was another tragedy waiting in the future, though. In June 2013, his adopted daughter Charlotte was to die of the same cancer that had killed her mother. 'Our hearts are heavy with the loss of our beautiful dear girl,' Pierce told reporters.

The years just before Cassie's death marked a wilderness in Pierce's career, with mixed reviews for *The Fourth Protocol*, *Taffin* and *The Deceivers*. But it was *Mister Johnson* that revived Pierce's spirits. It was reported that at the royal premiere, Queen Elizabeth found the film so moving she shed a tear. Pierce Brosnan was moving closer to working for Her Majesty, if the Fates allowed it this time.

In April 1994, Timothy Dalton, always a peculiar choice for Bond, announced that he was leaving the role. All sorts of names were being touted in one of cinema's favourite parlour games. Mel Gibson got a look in, as did Northern Irish actor Liam Neeson, whose debonair turn as Oskar Schindler brought him into the fold. But the smart money was on Pierce, whose good looks were helping him to poll well in market research on who should be the next Bond. Used to disappointment, Pierce held his fire and his breath until the phone rang. Which it did, at 12.35pm on 1 June 1994. At the other end was Pierce's agent, the wonderfully auspiciously named Fred Spector, who began the conversation with 'Hello Mr Bond, you've got the part.'

Within the week, 350 reporters from around the world gathered at London's salubrious Landmark Hotel. At the appointed hour, the James Bond theme music started to play and Pierce Brosnan emerged to the white light of camera flashes. It was happening at last. Pierce was Bond. 'I didn't think twice,' he answered when asked about taking the job. 'It was unfinished business.'

Before the first scene was shot, Pierce made it clear that he wouldn't be giving up his slight Irish lilt in order to play the quintessentially British spy. He reasoned that 'Sean Connery is Scottish and kept his accent so I'll keep mine.' And with that, the cameras started rolling on *GoldenEye*.

Pierce always looked as if he was born to play Bond, and as *GoldenEye* proceeded, it became clear that he was made for the part. Suave, smart and debonair, this was Fleming's literary hero incarnate. Pierce avoided late nights and all the messing that can distract an actor on set, preferring to paint, do yoga and play his clarinet. As to his performance? The audience lapped it up and Pierce was signed up for two more adventures. As a present to himself, he visited Christie's, the famous London auction house, where he bid on and bought the gold-plated typewriter that Ian Fleming had treated himself to after finishing his first draft of *Casino Royale* back in 1952. It cost the actor £52,500. He had come a long way from begging for a bank loan.

By the time of Pierce's second turn as Bond in *Tomorrow Never Dies* (1997), his portrayal was being widely lauded. The guy was a natural. Next up was *The World Is Not Enough* (1999), an expensive spectacular that featured the first female in a lead villain's role, with Sophie Marceau playing Elektra King. While the film did well at cinemas, at forty-six years of age Pierce was concerned that he was getting too old for the part and kept his options open by making films like *The Thomas Crown Affair* (1999) in tandem with his life as Bond. The rumour mill was busy but all talk ceased when it was announced that Pierce would play Bond once more in *Die Another Day* (2002). It was to be the last time he appeared as 007.

Producers were on the hunt for the next Bond despite the fact that the four films Pierce starred in were the highest grossing in the series since it started. They wanted a man aged between twenty-eight and thirty-two, with Jude Law, Clive Owen and Eric Bana all being mooted for the part. For his part, Pierce suggested that fellow Irishman Colin Farrell would 'eat the head off them all' if he got the job. In the end, Daniel Craig passed the test and continues to thrill when the script is right.

Pierce was the most suave of all the Bonds and definitely left his mark. Maybe in the next edition of this book, there'll be an addendum to this chapter when Michael Fassbender takes over as the second Irishman to become Bond. Personally, I'd love to see that – but I can die happy now that Pierce has had his shot.

*　　*　　*

I've tried several times to get Pierce on the *Late Late Show* when he's back in Ireland but so far he has eluded me. He's way up at the top of my wishlist, partly because of his wry sense of humour. There's a great advert on Irish TV in which he takes the mickey out of himself. He's standing in the street talking to a crowd of people, saying 'It's nice to be back in Ireland', when he realizes they aren't paying any attention to him because they're looking over his shoulder at a poster for Sky Broadband! It's this humour as well as his looks that made him such a perfect Bond. Not everyone back in Ireland would have been aware that he was Irish when he got the job but they were more than happy to take the credit!

I can't see them giving up on Bond films any time soon. The formula changes subtly with each change of lead actor – the overt sexism has gone, while there is less racial stereotyping of men with phoney Eastern European accents – but there are still plenty of sexy women, gory deaths, and races to save the world from imminent destruction. New generations of children are discovering Bond, as the fast pace and multiple explosions are well able to compete with Xbox and PlayStation for their attention. And long may it continue! It's a terrific business model . . .

And in my last chapter, I'm going to have a look at how the Irish have fared in the British business world, from their inauspicious start at the bottom of the social heap to the heady heights they've now attained. You could say we're 'high-flyers'.

12

THE BUSINESSMEN

THE IRISH IMMIGRANTS of the mid-twentieth century were mostly underdogs in society, doing menial work without getting a chance to step on to the career ladder that would allow them to raise their standard of living. There was a lot of infrastructure building going on in Britain – of housing, schools, hospitals and roads – and that's where many of them earned their crust. However, as the years went on the canny ones learned the trade and managed to start their own companies. In the present day, there are dozens of multi-million-pound Irish construction firms in the UK. These include Laing O'Rourke, responsible for building Heathrow Terminal 5 and the new stand at Ascot; the O'Rourke part of the company was started in 1977 by Ray O'Rourke from County Mayo. There's John Murphy & Sons, who worked on the Channel Tunnel Rail Link and the Olympic Park; it was started by John Murphy from Kerry who came over to Britain before the Second World War. And McNicholas Construction, headed by Tommy McNicholas from County Mayo, has been working on British utilities, roads and rail networks since the 1940s. The Irish are now said to own 10 per cent of the UK's lucrative building trade – so they've come a long way from David Kelly's 'O'Reilly the builder' in *Fawlty Towers*!

Building is not the only type of business the Irish have infiltrated though. You'll find Irish CEOs at the top of many UK-based firms, and many businesses that were started in Ireland have crossed the water to bring their services to UK consumers. When the *Irish Post* ran a supplement in July 2013 on the Top 100 Irish businesses in Britain, they were spoilt for choice. Here's my selection of some of the most influential.

ARTHUR GUINNESS: thirst-quencher
1725–23 January 1803

Guinness is good for you.
– advertising slogan, 1920s

It's not very politically correct to sing the praises of booze but anyone who has sat at a barstool in good company and picked up their first pint of fresh, creamy Guinness will know that, sometimes, life is just grand. Guinness drinkers like to talk about where to get the best pint (Galway) and what constitutes a fine pint (creamy rings all the way down the glass) and even the glass itself comes up for discussion (much talk of the dreadful 'lager'-style glass foisted upon us recently!). Once the chat about the state of the pint ends, the conversation moves on and the evening begins. Poor Arthur rarely gets a mention.

Young Arthur Guinness grew up in Celbridge, County Kildare, where his father was steward to an estate belonging to the Archbishop of Cashel. He learned about brewing at his father's knee and when the Archbishop died and left him £100 in his will, Arthur set up his own small brewery, which he left his brother to run. In 1759, he took out a lease on a disused brewery in St James's Gate, Dublin, and began successfully brewing ale, using the area's great source of pure water.

In the 1770s, a new darker drink called 'porter' arrived from London, a type of beer that was popular with the English capital's street and river porters. Arthur must have formed a liking for it because he hastily switched production to make his own porter at the Dublin premises and never looked back. He exported his own version, made with his special Dublin water, back to London and it soon achieved fame over there, becoming more popular than the original version.

As a businessman, Arthur could be tough if he had to. When the sheriff came to cut off his access to water in a legal dispute, Arthur saw him off with a pickaxe. And he campaigned vociferously to reduce the tax on Irish beer, which was set at a higher rate than its English equivalents. Meanwhile, he found time to have twenty-one children with his wife Olivia (of whom only ten survived to adulthood), and he was an active member of the community, a governor of the Meath Hospital and Secretary to the Friendly Brothers of St Patrick.

Ask people in the twenty-first century to name a famous Irish export and Guinness will still be top of the list for most. That inheritance Arthur received would fund umpteen generations of his family down through the centuries.

But is Guinness actually good for you, as the old advertising slogan claimed? They've long since stopped using it, because it's against the law to make health claims without scientific evidence to back them up. But does it make you feel good? As my old dad always said, 'in moderation'.

JOHN PHILIP HOLLAND: submarine inventor

29 February 1840–12 August 1914

> Sometimes she doesn't work perfectly, but often she does, and I don't think in the present emergency we can afford to let her slip.
>
> – President Theodore Roosevelt

Life could have been very different, not just for John Philip Holland but also for the world of warfare, if the Clare man had stayed on his chosen path in life as a Christian Brother.

Born in Liscannor, County Clare, Holland was a smart student with a particular interest in science. He began teaching for the Christian Brothers but got sick and was released from his initial vows, thereby making him a layman by the time he headed for Boston in 1873.

While in the United States, Holland continued the work he had started in Ireland: inventing a contraption that could sail under the sea, which he called a 'submarine'. By 1875, he was confident enough to offer his patent to the US Navy but they turned him down, dismissing the invention as 'a fantastic scheme of a civilian landsman'.

A product of his time, religiously and politically, Holland was not a fan of Great Britain and blamed that country for the pains suffered in his own. He argued that as long as Britannia ruled the waves, Ireland would remain downtrodden and oppressed and gave his support to emigrant rebels. In fact, his work on the submarine was funded by the Fenian Brotherhood (they called it the 'Fenian Ram') but they fell out and parted company in 1881 when the costs of the inventor's constant tinkering became too much for them to fathom. Holland went his own way and ended up working as an engineer while continuing to harbour dreams of nautical greatness.

Eventually, in 1897, the *Holland VI* saw the light of day. It was the first submarine that could travel submerged for any distance, by combining electric motors for use under the water and petrol-powered engines for use above the waves. It was still imperfect but the navy chiefs knew they couldn't afford to pass it up. They bought it for $150,0000 and renamed it the USS *Holland*. Thereafter it became the prototype for the US Navy's submarine fleet – and for most other navies round the world.

There was, no doubt, a bitter irony for Holland when his company sold the submarine plans to the British Admiralty – the last people he would ever have wanted to benefit from his invention. Still, business is business and they say everything is for sale . . .

Holland died in August 1914, just as the dogs of war were unleashed on a brittle world. He didn't live to see the full potential of his invention, be it for pain or peace.

HORSE RACING: Ireland's national sport

> [Ireland] in its small compass contains a larger percentage
> of horse-lovers than any country on the face of the earth.
> – *Irish Times*, 1907

Anyone who visits the racecourses of Britain will be aware how much the Irish are involved both on and off the track, because there will be Irish accents all around you. The Irish contribution to racing in Britain is lucrative, powerful – and occasionally controversial.

There are too many people associated with this story to mention all of them, but it would be remiss not to talk about the likes of Vincent O'Brien, the Irish trainer who won the Aintree Grand National three times in a row, starting with Early Mist (1953), then Royal Tan (1954) and finally Quare Times in 1955. O'Brien was responsible for training Hatton's Grace, one (between 1949 and 1951) of only five horses to win three consecutive Cheltenham Champion Hurdles. In partnership with Lester Piggott (whose daughter is now a correspondent for RTÉ Sport), O'Brien won two Prix de l'Arcs in 1977 and 1978 – and that's just a flavour of the success he experienced in his long life. Such was the esteem in which he was held, at the time of his death at the age of ninety-two in 2009, O'Brien was voted by readers of the *Racing Post* as the greatest, most influential racing figure of all time.

Another key Irish figure in the equine world of Anglo-Irish racing has the very same surname as the man above but is no relation. The physically diminutive but professionally imposing figure of Aidan O'Brien has dominated the tracks and fields of Ireland and Britain for the best part of the past twenty years. O'Brien is one of very few European trainers to have saddled more than 240 winners in a calendar year. His wins over his career include hatfuls of Irish and English classics, and, until 2013, he appeared to have established a monopoly on the Curragh Derby in recent times – he hasn't done too badly at Epsom either, and trained Camelot, the winner of both Derbys in 2012.

Equally impressive is the colourful career of Kieren Fallon, County Clare man, son of a plasterer and from a family with no connections to the equine world. Fallon has been champion jockey for three consecutive years (1997–9), winning 202, 204 and 202 races in each year respectively. He would be champion jockey again in

2001 and 2002 before completing the sextet in 2003. Known as the Assassin, Fallon has had his fair share of controversy. Accusations of race-fixing were thrown out of court following a lengthy and widely reported court case. Positive drug testing led to Fallon being banned and so the 'colourful' tag stuck. Recent years have seen Fallon stage something of a comeback with wins at the Oaks d'Italia (2010) and the German Oaks (Preis der Diana) in 2011.

It would be remiss to mention the men but not their trusty steeds of which there are so many legendary monikers that a mere list of names would suffice. However, let's just single out the likes of Sadler's Wells (champion sire in UK and Ireland fourteen times), Arkle (Cheltenham Gold Cup winner 1964, 1965 and 1966) and Dawn Run (Gold Cup winner in 1986). Then there's the unlucky Shergar, record-breaking winner of the Epsom Derby in 1981, who was stolen two years later and has never been found, spawning umpteen books and films over the years, each with their own theory as to who was responsible.

Huge sums of money are generated from the breeding and training of horses, but cash also changes hands at the bookies, and the Irish company Paddy Power has soaked up its share of punters' bets in the UK. Started in 1988 in Ireland, it soon had branches across Britain with its trademark green frontage and tongue-in-cheek 'Paddy' name. They gained notoriety for novelty bets on things that are no joking matter, such as the extinction of polar bears and a rather dodgy one about whether Barack Obama would finish his first term of office, which was widely interpreted as speculation on whether he would be assassinated. But the boys in green continued undaunted and in 2011 they came sixth in the *Management Today* list of 'Britain's most admired companies'. So they must be doing something right.

Anything to do with horses and you'll find an Irishman some-where behind the scenes (if not in front of them). In 1673, Sir William Temple wrote to King Charles II that 'Horses in Ireland are a drug'. In my opinion, very little has changed in the intervening 340 years.

Now, from flying over jumps to transporting frequent flyers . . .

WILLIE WALSH: the Slasher
Born 25 October 1961

A reasonable man gets nowhere in negotiations.

Willie Walsh appears to have been a young man in a hurry with an ambition and ability to match that haste. Born in Dublin, he didn't waste time with higher education, going straight into a job as a cadet pilot with Ireland's national airline, Aer Lingus. He was a captain by 1990 and starting to dip a toe into management circles. By 2000, Walsh was chief operating officer of the airline and just a short time later, days before his fortieth birthday, he was made chief executive. Pretty good going in anyone's book.

The company faced a deep financial crisis but Walsh cut 2,500 jobs and tightened the belt, managing to turn round the loss-making airline by 2004, when it posted a €107 million profit. Aer Lingus was now the most profitable state-owned airline in the world.

It wasn't long before bigger guns came calling and Walsh duly jumped ship (or rather plane!) and became chief executive of British Airways in October 2005 when they needed him to sort out their own money worries. He gained the nickname 'Slasher' for his economies but I can't imagine he was losing any sleep over it. There were plenty of other things to worry about: increasing oil prices, competition from low-cost carriers such as that of his compatriot Michael O'Leary (see below), snow, ice and – to top it all – volcanic ash from Iceland!

When BA joined with Iberia to form IAG, there was only one man for the top job, a position Walsh assumed in January 2011. This role sees Walsh oversee nearly 400 planes flying to over 200 destinations and carrying more than 69 million passengers every year.

A self-confessed workaholic, Walsh has often said that he intends to retire at fifty-five: 'I'd always had that as a target for myself. I don't know why. I was seventeen when I started in Aer Lingus. I've worked quite hard over the years.'

At rising fifty-two, the baby-faced boss has just over three years to go at the time of writing. Only a fool would bet on him pulling the escape cord so soon . . .

MICHAEL O'LEARY: the 'jumped-up paddy'
Born 20 March 1961

I don't give a shite if nobody likes me.

Michael O'Leary is a loudmouth who very often talks a lot of sense. He's forever popping up on British and Irish TV news to criticize whoever happens to be standing in the way of his low-cost airline Ryanair at that time: the big airlines, airport operators, politicians, the Green movement or Britain's air traffic control system (which he describes as 'poxy'). He's clashed with a disabled man who had the cheek to ask that he supply a wheelchair, and his own staff, who are forbidden from charging their mobile phones at work and have to bring in their own pens. But for millions of fans, he's the man who made weekend breaks affordable, allowed British people to reach their second homes in the South of France, and brought over the Polish builders to finish patios all over Britain.

Born in Mullingar, County Westmeath, to a well-off farming family, he was schooled at Clongowes Wood College, which is like Ireland's version of Eton, before studying at Trinity College Dublin. He worked in a tax consultancy, set up a couple of newsagents' shops and was then employed in an aircraft leasing company, where he studied the model of a low-cost airline in America before landing at Ryanair in 1991. From there the only way was up as he cut back on all the 'frills' of travel in order to slash ticket prices as far as possible.

Happy to characterize himself as a 'jumped-up paddy', O'Leary is a great self-publicist with a keen eye for a headline – as when he promised that business-class passengers would receive 'free beds and blowjobs'. He brings entertainment to the serious world of aviation and if it's notoriously difficult to get the cheapest of the cheap flights he advertises without standing on your head and waggling your ears while reciting Hail Marys backwards, so be it. He's made it cheaper and easier for the Irish to come to Britain and vice versa, and the more we interact, the more opportunities for both to benefit. So that's why I couldn't possibly leave Michael O'Leary out of this book.

When he appeared on the *Late Late Show*, O'Leary was an engaging, enraging guest who described pilots as 'overpaid taxi drivers'. Shortly after his appearance, he sent me a letter in which he suggested that Ryanair and my show had much in common in that people love to give out about it but tend to watch all the same . . . A big man with a big mouth, I suspect there's a big heart in there despite all the bluster.

*   *   *

So there you have it: Irish émigrés have not only brought you culture and entertainment but we've invaded the UK business world as well. London hosts umpteen Irish business networking groups with annual dinners and meet-and-greet events, and makes billions of pounds of revenue from their big corporations.

According to surveys, Irish accents give you an advantage in the business world over English ones, so long as they are gentle and not difficult to understand. Perhaps it's because a poll found that women think Irish accents are the world's sexiest, with Italian second and Scottish third. That's a huge sea change from the 'No dogs, no blacks, no Irish' signs of the 1950s! Landladies didn't want us in their beds back then, but now it seems things could be a little different.

Change didn't happen simply because of one or two handsome actors or charismatic figureheads. It was a long time coming for many different reasons, and in the final chapter of the book I'll sum up what I think brought about the newly warm and cosy relationship that both nations enjoy in the twenty-first century.

CONCLUSION

IN THE SUMMER OF 2013, when Gaelic football teams from all over Ireland competed for provincial glory, one surprise success story was the emergence of London as a team to be reckoned with. Such is the growth of Gaelic football in the UK that London has been part of the competition for some years now. The reason for this unlikely success is that lots of young Irish people are on the move. The economic downturn has emptied towns and villages around Ireland of their young, many of whom have travelled to Dublin, London, Brisbane and Ottawa. In London, the reception they've received has been completely different from that their forefathers experienced in the 1950s. This generation are educated, open-minded and ambitious. They can fly home regularly and Skype every day: it's a very different life for the twenty-first-century economic migrant. There's no begrudging, since they come to Britain as equals to live and work on a level playing field.

Naturally, there's disgust directed towards the bankers and politicians who got us into this mess, but that's true on both sides of the Irish Sea. In some ways, the recession brought our two countries closer by underlining our mutual economic dependence. Britain couldn't afford to let Irish banks fail any more than we could have coped with British banks failing. It's just one more post-peace-process phenomenon that has strengthened the bond of friendship between the two countries.

I also feel it's important to emphasize once more how much the Queen's visit to Ireland in May 2011 meant. It may not have had the same resonance in the UK but at home it was enormous. She'd been on the throne for fifty-nine years and visited over a hundred countries round the world without being able to come to the one in her own backyard. At the time it was suggested that for the Queen, that visit was like 'a little girl with a big garden she could never go and look at. She couldn't even peek through the gate to see what the neighbours looked like.' And then when she did come she really dazzled, from the moment she stepped off the plane in an emerald green coat. It felt like a very distinctive line in the sand, and we were delighted one and all that the visit went off so well.

The month before that, all those hidden royal watchers in Ireland came out of the shadows and traffic ground to a halt when William and Kate got married. I remember the morning well as I called in on my mum, who was having a breakfast with friends to watch the ceremony. If her father, an ardent republican, only knew! At RTÉ, I looked around and most of my colleagues were glued to the various television screens around the place, watching the event for 'research purposes', and we talked about it on that Friday's *Late Late Show*. Even the birth of Prince George garnered plenty of media coverage as the young royals have really gone from being 'just' monarchy to full-blown global 'celebs'.

The peace process looms large in this story and all the people who worked towards it over the decades, both in front of and behind the scenes, can take credit for the change. I also believe that hardened attitudes were chipped away by the public – and lesser-known – figures I've mentioned in this book. How could anyone claim the Irish were all bad when they were watching Terry Wogan working his magic on the television or humming along to Val Doonican? Every single book, song, joke and play that crossed the water contributed to greater understanding of the Irish character. When Dave Allen described his upbringing by nuns, when Richard Harris was outrageous on the *Parkinson* show, or when Vincent O'Brien won the Grand National three times in a row, they all made their mark and the British took note.

I've had my own little forays into the world of British radio in recent years and it's been an adventure but it's also quite daunting to broadcast to the bigger audience. I can understand why my compatriots in the media have been tempted across over the years but, having said that, I'm a home bird. I like my local pub, and I love being able to jump into the car and drive across to the west coast for a weekend. It's the draw of the land and its history, a sense of not wanting to divest yourself of all that – that's what keeps the Irish at home.

But then again, the 2011 census in Britain found that Irish people who live in the UK are less likely to identify themselves as British than any other ethnic group. No matter how long they spend in Britain – even after decades – they still maintain their sense of Irish identity, and hang on to their Irish passports. Maybe it's because we're such a small nation that we feel so strongly about it. Fortunately, you can pack Ireland in your luggage and bring it with you. That's what most of the Irish in this book did. They may have left Ireland but Ireland never left them.

I end by saluting the great Irish men and women who have flown the flag for their country with determination, dexterity and dignity. From the maids at big houses to the Tube builders and street cleaners and on to the entertainers and stars who made it all the way to the top. To the countless people I've omitted, I apologize and ask that you take my selection as a small representation of a much bigger story.

ACKNOWLEDGEMENTS

I'M ALWAYS ASKED where I get the time to read let alone *write* a book and the answer is Monday afternoons. That is the only time I can disappear to whatever library hasn't been closed down to scribble as many thoughts as possible until the following week. This has meant way too much time away from my day jobs. My friends on *Tubridy*, the radio show on RTÉ 2FM, are like extended family and didn't mind my absences too much. I can rant away unimpeded and they laugh dutifully at all my 'jokes'. Dave, G1, G2, Lorraine, Jack and Paul, thank you. On the *Late Late Show*, they could have done with more of me and I appreciate their patience and hard work. I'm back now. Thank you.

Martin Redfern inherited this book and kept the faith. Moira Reilly is a wonderful force of nature in Ireland's book world and I'm lucky to have her by my side. Thank you.

Andrea Pappen and Gill Paul were enormously helpful, digging up facts and figures to help a wayward soul. You both deserve better than me and you have it now! Thank you.

Noel Kelly and Niamh Kirwan fight the fires and keep the peace. Thank you.

My brothers and sisters, Judith, Niall, Rachel and Garrett are the sounding boards of sanity on whom I count and whom I love. Thank you

Aoibhinn, the lady whose elegance is unsurpassed and whose support is inestimable. Mo Ghrá. Thank you.

My most beautiful girls who tolerate bits of paper, random facts, Post-its and a visit to yet another bookshop – Ella and Julia, they haven't invented a word to describe how much I love you both. Thank you.

My Dad and my Mum, who gave me a love of history and humour, of people and politics, of art and words. I'm sorry Dad won't be reading this but he'd probably have preferred the crossword. Mum continues to be my cheerleader-in-chief. I dedicate this book to you both. For everything, thank you.

NOTES

THE HELLRAISERS
A 2009 survey ...: Deirdre Mongan,
  Ann Hope and Mairea Nelson, 'Social
  consequences of harmful use of alcohol in
  Ireland', Health Research Board Overview
  Series, 2009.
RICHARD HARRIS
'If I win an award ...': *Irish Times*,
  28 October 2002.
'One day was luxury ...': Robert Sellers,
  *An A–Z of Hellraisers: A Comprehensive
  Compendium of Outrageous Sobriety*,
  London: Preface, 2010, p. 14.
'I wanted to embrace it all ...': Ibid, p. 33.
He was lucky to survive ...: Dennis Pringle,
  'The resurgence of tuberculosis in the
  Republic of Ireland: perceptions and
  reality', *Social Science and Medicine* 68(4),
  2009, pp. 620–4.
'I look f**king fifty ...': Sellers, *An A–Z of
  Hellraisers*, p. 43.
'I have made seventy movies ...': Ibid, p. 209.
'Father, if you are going to hear my
  confession ...': Ibid, p. 202.
'I treated them ...': Ibid, p. 219.
'How about Sherlock O'Holmes ...': Ibid,
  p. 240.
'I'm very sorry Ray McAnally died ...':
  Sunday Independent, 27 October 2002.
'Why the f**k ...': Sellers, *An A–Z of
  Hellraisers*, p. 249.
The 90s proved fertile ground ...: Ibid,
  p. 268.
'If you're paying the mortgage ...': Ibid,
  p. 268.

'Richard was regaling us ...': Ibid, p. 269.
'Actors take themselves so seriously ...': *Daily
  Telegraph*, 28 October 2002.
PETER O'TOOLE
'God, you can love it! ...': Sellers, *An A–Z of
  Hellraisers*, p. 236.
Not unlike Richard Harris ...: Ibid, p. 17.
'They tore up my drawing ...': Peter O'Toole,
  Loitering with Intent, vol. 1: *The Child*,
  London: Pan, 1993, p. 17.
'They were shocked ...': Sellers, *An A–Z of
  Hellraisers*, p. 18.
'I soon found out ...': Ibid, p. 26.
'I'd have made ...': Ibid, p. 59.
'Oh darling ...': Ibid, pp. 82–3.
'I woke up one morning ...': Ibid.
'Make the world your ashtray ...': Ibid,
  pp. 234, 237.
'I do not regret one drop ...': *Observer*,
  21 January 2007.
'Came the morning, ...': *Guardian*, 19 March
  2003.
He later said ...: *The Film Programme*, BBC
  Radio 4, 26 January 2007.
'He delivers every line ...': Michael
  Billington, *One Night Stands: A Critic's
  View of Modern British Theatre*, London:
  Nick Hern Books, rev. edn, 2001.
'wretchedly inconsiderate': *Observer*,
  21 January 2007.
'At the end of the picture ...': Sellers, *An A–Z
  of Hellraisers*, p. 74.
JONATHAN RHYS MEYERS
'My favourite actors ...': *Daily Mirror*,
  25 April 2007.

'She drank her dole money ...': *News of the World*, 25 November 2007.

'What boy is not going to say ...': *Sunday Telegraph*, 27 January 2008.

'It was just the whole atmosphere ...': Ibid.

'Overnight success ...': *Los Angeles Times*, 18 November 2007.

'I am not a hellraiser ...': *Daily Mirror*, 25 April 2007.

'People have said ...': *Sunday Telegraph*, 27 January 2008.

'like having sex ...': *Ellen DeGeneres Show*, 15 January 2012.

'I kind of like ...': *Mail Online*, 12 June 2013.

THE COMEDIANS

DAVE ALLEN

'I'm bothered by power ...': *Daily Telegraph*, 12 March 2005.

'the Gestapo in drag': gleaned from the *Dictionary of Irish Biography* at http://dib.cambridge.org

'I arrived at this convent ...': Graham McCann, ed., *The Essential Dave Allen*, London: Hodder & Stoughton, 2005, p. 48.

'talking to God's middle-man, ...': Carolyn Soutar, *Dave Allen: The Biography*, London: Orion, 2005.

'Yes, of course he gets attacked ...': *Irish Times*, 17 January 1977.

Allen returned to Australia ...: television heaven.co.uk/daveallen.htm

'I'm still retired, ...': televisionheaven.co.uk/daveallen.htm

'We spend our lives ...': McCann, *The Essential Dave Allen*, p. 32.

'I don't know ...': *Daily Telegraph*, 12 March 2005.

'a torchbearer ...': *Irish Times*, 12 March 2005

DYLAN MORAN

'You're all talking shite ...': www.dylanmoran rules.com/TheGiftOfTheGag.html

'You know when you're late ...': Ibid.

'In Ireland ...': Ibid.

'The most fun I had, ...': Ibid.

FATHER TED

'The show's ...': Dermot Morgan, *Independent*, 2 March 1998.

DARA O BRIAIN

'This is the first time ...': *Irish Independent*, 15 September 2007.

'You're sitting next door ...': Author interview, London, 2012.

'Darby Brown, ...': Chortle.co.uk/interviews/2006/12/04/4772/ditzy

'It's easier to become well known ...': Author interview, London, 2012.

'There is a weird notion ...': Ibid.

Dara gigs in both countries ...: *Irish Times*, 7 August 1999.

'I think it's exceptionally rude ...': Author interview, London, 2012.

'Because I work so often ...': Ibid.

'You kind of have to lose ...': Ibid.

'given my education, ...': *Irish Times*, 7 August 1999.

THE CHAT SHOW HOSTS

EAMON ANDREWS

'He was born to blush ...': Tom Brennand, *Eamonn Andrews*, London: Weidenfeld & Nicolson, 1989, p. 3.

'A constant stream ...': Eamonn Andrews, *This Is My Life: The Autobiography*, London: Macdonald, 1963, p. 81.

'He sells an ordinariness. ...': Brennand, *Eamonn Andrews*, p. 9.

When the tape ...: Ibid, p. 47.

'Your Majesty ...': Ibid, p. 17.

'He brought to the business ...': *Irish Times*, 6 November 1987.

'Eamonn, clutching the big red book ...': *The Times*, 6 November 1987.

TERRY WOGAN

'Heard the one about the Irishman ...': Allison Pearson, *Irish Independent*, 12 September 2009.

'good timing ...': *Irish Times*, 3 November 1988.

'Blind faith ...': Terry Wogan, *Mustn't Grumble*, London: Orion, 2007, pp. 14–15.

'a little above average ...': Ibid, p. 19.

'What I think ...': Author interview, London, 26 August 2012.

'Every brief-less barrister ...': Ibid.

'the falling shreds ...': Ryan Tubridy, *JFK in Ireland: Four Days that Changed a President*, London: HarperCollins, 2010, p. 102.

'It had struck me ...': Author interview, London, 26 August 2012.

'I came to a realization ...': Ibid.

'I couldn't see ...': Ibid.

'I've never believed ...': Wogan, *Mustn't Grumble*, p. 39.

'The only thing ...': *Irish Times*, 27 February 2010.

'I think it was George Bernard Shaw ...': Author interview, London, 26 August 2012.

'While the masked man ...': *Irish Independent*, 7 December 1991.

'All the traffic stopped ...': Author interview, London, 26 August 2012.

'It has to look easy ...': *Irish Times*, 3 November 1988.

'She [Davis] could never understand ...': *Irish Times*, 27 February 2010.

'the Irish and English ...': *Irish Times*, 3 November 1988.

'Terry Wogan is not a major talent ...': *Irish Independent*, 8 January 1986.

'When we were growing up': *Irish Times*, 27 February 2010.

'Bow the head ...': *Daily Telegraph*, 12 December 2005.

'Limerick never left me; ...': *Irish Times*, 12 May 2007.

'One of the more hurtful ...': Wogan, *Mustn't Grumble*, p. 54.

GRAHAM NORTON

'When I left Ireland ...': Author interview, November 2012.

'Childhood: dull. ...': Graham Norton, *So Me*, London: Hodder and Stoughton, 2005, p. 3.

'I was ... bored stiff ...': Author interview, November 2012.

'Maybe I would have enjoyed it more ...': Alison Bowyer, *Graham Norton Laid Bare*, London: André Deutsch, 2002, p. 22.

'It never really crossed my mind ...': *Irish Times*, 30 January 2010.

'Ireland was an impossible place ...': Bowyer, *Graham Norton Laid Bare*, p. 46.

'Irish twenty, ...': Ibid, p. 60.

'San Francisco ...': *Observer*, 18 November 2007.

'The whole idea of Ireland ...': Author interview, November 2012.

'with his eye-rolling expressions ...': Bowyer, *Graham Norton Laid Bare*, p. 107.

'I really am terrified ...': *Irish Times*, 27 February 1999.

'You know what they always say ...': Ibid.

'Whereas any British performer ...': Author interview, November 2012.

'a 21st-century Larry Grayson ...': Bowyer, *Graham Norton Laid Bare*, p. 13.

'That salary is a miracle. ...': *Observer*, 18 November 2007.

'Almost as soon as we got back ...': Norton, *So Me*, p. 231.

'As I get older ...': Author interview, November 2012.

'I always say ...': *Observer*, 18 November 2007.

DES LYNAM

'A common misperception ...': *Independent*, 6 October 2005.

'I had a very good life ...': Author interview, November 2012.

'I didn't go to school ...': Ibid.

'The teacher said, ...': Des Lynam, *I Should Have Been at Work!*, London: HarperCollins, 2005, p. 7.

'I used to cry ...': Author interview, November 2012.

'He is neither urban nor rural ...': *Sunday Times*, 8 August 1999.

'the menopausal woman's ...': *Daily Mail*, 4 October 1999.

'Being Irish puts things into perspective. ...': Ibid.

'There have been three great white entertainers, ...': *Sunday Times*, 8 August 1999.

'It may seem odd ...': Ibid.

ZIG AND ZAG

'Never mind the zogabongs ...': Zogabongs are the furry pom-poms attached to their heads; Zig's are red and Zag's are yellow, in case you ever need to tell them apart.

POLITICIANS, SOLDIERS AND REPORTERS

EDMUND BURKE

'The only thing necessary ...': Quote often attributed to Burke although it is not found in his writings.

BRENDAN BRACKEN

'Everything about you is phoney ...': Acquaintance of Brendan Bracken, quoted in Charles Lysaght, 'Churchill's Favourite Chela', *History Today*, 52, 2, February 2002.

'I looked it up ...': From Bracken Memorial Lecture by Charles Lysaght, winstonchurchill.org.

'the fantasist whose fantasies ...': Ibid.

'The blackshirts of God ...': Gleaned from the *Oxford Dictionary of National*

Biography, Oxford: Oxford University Press, 2004–12.

'quarrelled and argued incessantly . . .': Bracken Memorial Lecture by Charles Lysaght (winstonchurchill.org).

BRENDAN 'PADDY' FINUCANE

'If ever I feel a bitter feeling . . .': quoted in *Irish Times*, 14 July 2012.

'I shoot to hit the machine . . .': century-of-flight.net

'I've been blessed . . .': 'In Search of "Paddy" Finucane', Documentary on One, RTÉ, 2004.

'The cockpit was awash . . .': Ibid.

'Finucane Flies Again': century-of-flight.net

'drowned in the English Channel . . .': *Irish Independent*, 18 July 1942.

ORLA GUERIN

'I've found that people . . .': *London Evening Standard*, 10 April 2002.

'You . . . have to be very dedicated . . .': blogs. spokenword.ac.uk/cculle200/2011/11/30/ the-thrill-of-the-chaseorla-guerin-a-life-on-the-frontline/

'very, very strong links there': *Observer*, 28 August 2005.

THE ARTISTS

JOHN HENRY FOLEY

'He abandoned strict academic Neo-classicism . . .': John T. Turpin, 'The Career and Achievement of John Henry Foley, Sculptor (1818–1874)', *Dublin Historical Record*, 32, 2, March 1979, p. 42.

FRANCIS BACON

'That man who paints . . .': Obituary, *New York Times*, 29 April 1992.

PHILIP TREACY

'Give Philip a needle . . .': philiptreacy.co.uk

'I'd rather spend the money . . .': philiptreacy. co.uk

ORLA KIELY

'It was lovely . . .': Kate Burt, interview with Orla Kiely, *Independent*, 22 October 2010.

'I sometimes think that my brain . . .': Independent.co.uk

PAURIC SWEENEY

'Fashion cannot and must not . . .': Pauric Sweeney, fashionologie.com, 24 June 2009.

'Creatively, Ireland developed . . .': Sarah Haight, *W Magazine*, July 2010.

THE WRITERS

JONATHAN SWIFT

'Satire is a sort of glass . . .': Jonathan Swift, Preface, *The Battle of the Books*, 1704.

'I cannot but conclude . . .': Jonathan Swift, 'A Voyage to Brobdingnag', *Gulliver's Travels*, 1726, Part II, Chapter 7.

BRAM STOKER

'My revenge is just begun! . . .': Bram Stoker, *Dracula*, 1897.

OSCAR WILDE

'There is no sin . . .': Oscar Wilde, 'The Critic as Artist', Part II, in *Intentions*, 1891.

GEORGE BERNARD SHAW

'My way of joking . . .': George Bernard Shaw, *John Bull's Other Island*, 1904, Act II.

EDNA O'BRIEN

'A writer's life . . .': *Observer*, 6 February 2011.

'Exile and separation . . .': Interview at Edna O'Brien's publishers, 2012.

MARIAN KEYES

'What doesn't kill us . . .': Marian Keyes, *The Other Side of the Story*, London: Penguin Books, 2005, p. 105.

'We've even added some of our own words . . .': Gleaned from the *Oxford English Dictionary*.

THE THESPIANS

WILFRED BRAMBELL

'I hate your fucking cathedrals . . .': *Guardian*, 19 August 2002.

MICHAEL GAMBON

'I like being rough around the edges . . .': *Guardian*, 28 February 2004.

'coming back on holidays . . .': *Irish Times*, 24 April 2010.

'If you're at school . . .': *Irish Times*, 8 April 2006.

'I went, varoom!' . . .: Mel Gussow, *Michael Gambon: A Life in Acting*, New York: Applause, 2005, p. 32.

'I told him a lot of lies . . .': Ibid, p. 32

'O'Toole had just done *Lawrence of Arabia* . . .': *Observer*, 2 April 2000.

'We'd go to the pub . . .': *Observer*, 2 April 2000.

'Fundamentally, acting is a deep process . . .': Gussow, *Michael Gambon*, p. 21.

'The cliché of English actors . . .': Ibid, p. 23.

FIONA SHAW

'I live among the English . . .': Brad Balfour,

'Focus on *The Last September*: Fiona Shaw in Film and Theater', *Irish Connections*, 10 July 2002

'an abandoned English fort ...': *Independent*, 10 July 2013.

'There once was a demographic survey ...': Balfour, 'Focus on The Last September'.

CHRIS O'DOWD

'We all want to be Daniel Day Lewis ...': *Sunday Times*, 15 March 2009.

'I was the guy ...': *The Times*, 16 July 2011.

'I don't know whether ...': *Sunday Times*, 13 March 2011.

'and just blew us away ...': *People*, 22 January 2006.

'There are so many Irish people ...': *Sunday Times*, 15 March 2009.

'They say that the power ...': *Sunday Times*, 13 March 2011.

'If the audience ...': *Sunday Business Post*, 11 December 2011.

THE MUSICIANS

VAL DOONICAN

'There's still a hard core ...': Wogan, *Mustn't Grumble*, p. 200.

GILBERT O'SULLIVAN

'I write pop songs ...': *Gilbert O'Sullivan: Out on His Own*, BBC 4, 29 August 2011.

BOB GELDOF

'Did God knock on the wrong door ...': Mary Moriarty and Catherine Sweeney, *Bob Geldof*, Dublin: O'Brien, 1989, p. 75.

'Jagger fascinated me ...': Bob Geldof, *Is That It?*, London: Macmillan, 2012, p. 25.

'It was a nice way ...': Ibid, p. 61.

'people who were so shrunken ...': Ibid, p. 215.

THE BOY BANDS

LOUIS WALSH

'Deep down I am nice ...': *Independent*, 27 August 2006.

'If you could work with ...': *Sunday Mirror*, 11 August 2002.

'I didn't want to do that show ...': *Sunday Independent*, 9 August 2009.

'a tongue on him ...': Ibid.

'jumped-up karaoke singer ...': *Observer*, 1 December 2002.

'tried to ruin me ...': *Closer Magazine*

'Warhol and stuff': *The Times*, 20 August 2011.

'lots of acquaintances ...': Ibid.

'Retirement? No, ...': *Daily Mail*, 11 April 2011.

STEPHEN GATELY

'No marching or shouting ...': *The Times*, 11 October 2009.

NIALL HORAN

'Every now and then ...': Metro Lyrics blog, 1 February 2012.

'I was just clocking on ...': *Sun*, 16 April 2012.

One Direction's first single ...: *South Wales Echo*, 13 January 2012.

THE HARRY POTTER BUNCH

BRENDAN GLEESON

'It's the parents that spot me ...': *News of the World*, 19 June 2011.

'There were these fairly tough guys ...': *Independent*, 30 May 1988.

'too fat, too old ...': *Herald*, 12 April 2008.

'The car erupted ...': *York Press*, 31 August 2011.

'only this time I could do it ...': *The Times*, 14 July 2007.

'The kids were allowed ...': *Belfast Telegraph*.

DOMHNALL GLEESON

'Joining *Harry Potter* for the first time ...': *Sun*, 8 July 2011.

'[It] was kind of cool ...': Ibid.

'You know you have your top ten list ...': Ibid.

'I don't think Colin [Farrell] ...': Ibid.

DEVON MURRAY

'It's not like I try to blow things up ...': Devon Murray as Seamus Finnigan in *Harry Potter and the Goblet of Fire*, 2005.

'My character's a bit stupid ...': *Sunday Mirror*, 23 September 2001.

In other words, at just thirteen years old ...: *Mirror*, 16 December 2003.

'I took him under my wing ...': *Sun*, 21 September 2005.

'I'm still plain old Devon ...': *Sunday Mirror*, 23 September 2001.

EVANNA LYNCH

'I saw her. [She] got in my head ...': Charlie Rose, 'An Hour with J.K. Rowling', 19 October 2012.

'Don't be too hard on Termonfeckin ...': *Sunday Business Post*, 21 November 2010.

'The others could play Luna ...': Ibid.

'I don't think she's weird ...': *Irish Times*, 21 March 2011.

'I love that I get to keep ...': *Sun*, 11 July 2011.

THE JAMES BOND FRANCHISE
'We're looking for a new James Bond ...': *Observer*, 29 February 2004, and *Late Late Show*, 18 April 2010.
KEVIN McCLORY
'The Bond movies have made so much money ...': Patricia E. Keegan, 'Kevin McClory: James Bond Filmmaker', washingtoninternational.com
McClory got a job ...: Robert Sellers, *The Battle for Bond: The Genesis of Cinema's Greatest Hero*, Sheffield: Tomahawk Press, 2007, p. 13.
'What was easy at 40 ...': Ibid, p. 67.
'the exclusive right to use ...': *Independent*, 7 December 2006.
one report suggests ...: Sellers, *The Battle for Bond*, p. 207.
MARTIN GRACE
'The bravest man ...': *Daily Telegraph*, 2 April 2010.
'Emigration at that time ...': Clontubrid school project, 2006, q&a.
They only got permission ...: *The Times*, 27 February 2010.
And the high-speed car chase ...: *Irish Times*, 20 March 2010.
'very feeble, has back and neck problems ...': Clontubrid school project, 2006, q&a.
'The impact was so lightning fast ...': *The Times*, 27 February 2010.
'I never felt a stunt was scary ...': Clontubrid school project, 2006, q&a.
PIERCE BROSNAN
'[Brosnan] slots so naturally ...': Peter Carrick, *Pierce Brosnan*, London: Robert Hale, 2000, p. 154.
'dreadful human beings ...': *Observer*, 14 October 2001.
'My life in Ireland ...': York Membery, *Pierce Brosnan: The Biography*, London: Virgin, 1997, p. 9.
'When I arrived I somehow knew ...': Ibid, p. 18.

'I got ribbed a lot ...': Ibid, p. 19.
'I looked up at the big screen ...': Ibid, p. 18.
'I could act out all the stuff ...': Ibid, p. 33.
'Either I stayed in England ...': Ibid, p. 88.
'I felt very manipulated ...': Aine O'Connor (ed.), *Leading Hollywood*, Dublin: Wolfhound Press, 1996, p. 130.
'She never wanted to die ...': Ibid, p. 137.
'Hello Mr Bond ...': Membery, *Pierce Brosnan*, p. 165.
'I didn't think twice ...': Ibid, p. 164.
'Sean Connery is Scottish ...': Ibid, p. 168.
'eat the head off them all': *Guardian*, 2 November 2005.

THE BUSINESSMEN
JOHN PHILIP HOLLAND
'Sometimes she doesn't work perfectly ...': Edward C. Whitman, 'John Holland: Father of the Modern Submarine', *Undersea Warfare*, Summer 2003.
Holland died in August 1914 ...: Gleaned from the *Dictionary of Irish Biography* at http://dib.cambridge.org/
HORSE RACING
'[Ireland] in its small compass ...': *Racing the Irish Way: A Guide to Racing in Ireland*, at goracing.ie, p. 10.
'Horses in Ireland are a drug': *Racing the Irish Way: A Guide to Racing in Ireland*, p. 7.
WILLIE WALSH
A reasonable man gets nowhere ...': Comment made in staff publication when he was a representative of the Irish Airline Pilots' Association.
This role sees Walsh ...: iairgroup.com
MICHAEL O'LEARY
'I don't give a shite ...': *Guardian*, 24 June 2005.
a poll found that women ...: *Daily Telegraph*, 3 November 2009.

CONCLUSION
the 2011 census in Britain ...: *Belfast Telegraph*, 16 May 2013.